Michael

Happy birthday, 1988

with love,

Sheila & Henry

GREEK ISLAND COOKERY

GREEK ISLAND COOKERY

An evocation in words and watercolours

RENA SALAMAN & LINDA SMITH

EBURY PRESS
London

To Graeme
For his passion for the Greek Islands

Published by Ebury Press
Division of The National Magazine Company Ltd
Colquhoun House
27–37 Broadwick Street
London W1V 1FR

First impression 1987

ISBN 085223 621 2

Editor Suzanne Webber
Designer Roger Daniels

Computerset by MFK Typesetting Ltd., Hitchin, Hertfordshire
Printed and bound in Italy by New Interlitho, S.p.a., Milan

CONTENTS

INTRODUCTION

We are about to embark on a journey. The enormous sails already flapping like seagull wings against the breeze. A mythical journey, partly dream and partly reality. The travellers are jostling each other anxiously; protecting and counting time and again their ragged baggage; a couple of carton boxes tied with string, a *kourelou* (a typical striped Greek rug for laying out on the boat's deck), a brand new shopping bag from one of the large stores in metropolitan Athens, sparkling with colour and exuding alien affluence, perhaps containing the few bridal items necessary for the impending wedding, back on the island, of the only daughter of the household and guaranteed to impress the guests and achieve the final status symbol on the *proika* (dowry) provided by the parents.

The noise, the bustle, the whistling of boats, and the deafening hooting of taxis arriving to empty out more prospective travellers and add to the chaos. The inevitable sellers weave skilfully in and out of the crowd, offering their wares with a basket hanging over one arm. First comes the one with the cheese pies (tyropittes) in a glass contraption that keeps them warm with tiny charcoals burning in the tin tray underneath (there cannot be a journey in Greece without tyropittes); next comes the elderly *fystikas* (nut seller), who advertises with his hoarse voice that these are no ordinary nuts but the aristocratic breed from the island of Aegina, pistachio nuts. Then there is even the *lahiopolis* (the lottery seller). This is not very good ground for him, but who knows when good luck will strike, and besides he is an indispensable part of Greek life.

The feel, the air and excitement of the busy port emanates that familiar gripping longing for the places waiting to be reached, lying ahead, somewhere along the curving faint blue line of the sea merging with the horizon. The islands, that the Greek poet has likened to blooms floating in the Aegean: Santorini, Ios, Paros,

Naxos, Amorgos, Fourni, Sifnos, Tinos, Patmos, Kalymnos, Halki, Symi, Karpathos and one or two thousand more; some of them little more than mere dots in the blue vastness, a couple of rocks thrown together for the sake of Ulysses, to give him shelter from the wild, wrathful Sea-God, Poseidon (*Posithonas*).

As the glimmering white city is left behind, rooted in its Attic landscape, a mere hazy flat line reminding us of its presence, the travellers, by now, installed in their preferred positions, rugs spread on deck and valuable belongings by their side, feel relaxed enough suddenly to remember that in the bustle of the journey

LASTROS, CRETE

their appetite has been neglected. The inevitable parcel in a colourful napkin will unfold to spill its inevitable contents. First come the lemons, always at hand in case of rough seas – no one in Greece undertakes a sea journey without carrying along some lemons to be halved at the hour of need in order to smell them and bite into their refreshing rind. The food consists of suitably dry items specially selected from the Greek culinary *repertoire*: *keftethakia* (small fried herby hamburgers), green *dolmathakia* (stuffed vine leaves) with a Lenten stuffing of rice, onions, pine kernels and the aroma of the fields with quantities of slender green dill; a crusty loaf of bread; the ubiquitous startlingly ebony-polished olives, an uneven piece of cheese, perhaps the sharply savoury *lathotiri* from Mytilini, or the soft, deceptively creamy *kopanisti* from Mykonos, whose sharp peppery taste is unmatched by any other cheese; and, of course, a spring onion or two.

The family will dip into the meal, the children will be urged and shouted at and then it will be the turn of the immediate neighbours. The sacred offerings or *myrothies* as they are called in Greek, literally meaning 'samples to satisfy the nose', will be extended to the people nearby. The legendary Greek hospitality that has impressed travellers in the past few centuries is still at work!

In the islands, the poorest peasant will ask you into his clean and tidy cottage, give you cognac, coffee and a glass of water, after the invariable Greek fashion and offer you walnuts, which he will crack for you, or whatever else may be in season.

('GREEK LIFE IN TOWN AND COUNTRY', William Miller, George Newnes Ltd, London 1905.)

While you travel around the islands, the same hospitality will manifest itself in a handful of ways. An islander in his garden will probably offer you some fruit from his tree or the first of his pale lemons. During our travels, Linda and I were offered grapes, quinces, figs, pomegranates and oranges. Beyond a village along the hillsides, you may come across ladies clad in black collecting snails or most probably *horta* (wild greens) of various kinds according to the season. Among them will be dandelions, thin wild asparagus, young mustard plants, or young poppy plants, wild mint, sage or dill, a number of which are used to make the traditional local pies such as the *skaltsounakia* of Crete or the *lahanopittes* of Skopelos, Alonnisos or Skyros. On such an occasion in Crete, when we stopped to talk to two ladies stooped over the undergrowth, near the village of Aghios Vasilios, we were invited to sample a local speciality – a lunch of snails cooked with the heart-shaped leaves of a tender wild climber called *avronies*, which they were gathering. On another occasion near the village of Melabes we were offered the entire morning's crop of different wild greens, which are served boiled and dressed with aromatic local olive oil and lemon along with crispy fried squid, or small fish such as anchovies or whatever the fishing boats return with on that particular morning. And while Linda was painting the fishing boats in the harbour at Pigathia in Karpathos on a particularly cold and windy afternoon, she was brought a hot tea and a small glass of brandy from a house opposite. In the old city in Rhodes the local ladies protected her from cars trying to park where they would obstruct her view while painting.

In Santorini Maroulia Fytrou-Laoutha cooked the speciality of the island *domatokeftethes* for us to try. We were invited to people's houses to sample food or traditional cakes. In Mykonos we were invited to a local wedding, in Santorini to a *panegiris* (a celebration of a large family to honour Saint Dionysius in his church), which was followed after the liturgy by a feast in the churchyard with all kinds of fish and local red wine, singing and a lot of teasing. By 10 in the morning the spirits of the faithful were so high that I was proposed to by the 85-year-old wonderful-looking *pater familias* at the head of the table, who assured me that despite his age his heart was young. (I had no doubts either about his youthfulness or his vivacity!)

In the autumn, during that uniquely biblical task of the olive picking, if you stop and talk to the olive pickers, as we did in

Karpathos by the entrancing beach of Ammopi, you will almost
certainly be asked to join them in a picnic, even if that consists of
some hard, home-made island bread with its unique lightly sour
taste, the ubiquitous Greek olives, some salted sardines and an
onion or two. Poor islanders are not concerned or embarrassed
about *what* they offer you but the spirit in which the offering is
made. Later, in the olive mill at the village of Menetes, amidst the
deafening noise of the grinding, the pressing and the hissing of the
various machines, while olives were arriving by the sackful, more
olives were rinsed or crushed and in a corner thick-green olive oil
was spouting into a huge aluminium container, I was also asked,
despite the early hour of the visit, to join the men for an *ouzo*, green
olives and some bread which were spread on an inverted empty oil
drum that served as a table.

One cannot visit an island household without being offered
something to eat, to drink or to take with you. Consequently a
word that one hears a lot on Greek islands either at homes or
tavernas is *mezzes* (something to nibble at) or *mezethaki*, the second
being the diminutive form of the first. On Alonnisos, where we
spend our summers, on occasions when I have dropped by to see a
family at a time when a husband or a son has returned from a
particularly plentiful fishing expedition, I could not leave without
taking with me some of the catch, perhaps some newly-spawned
mackerel in August, some creamy-looking elegant squid, a small
octopus or two.

As you might expect, the food of the Greek islands revolves
round the sea like the lives of the islanders. Not only does it contain
silvery, pink or orange-coloured fish glistening with freshness, but
all kinds of seafood – from the ubiquitous, lustrous, spiky sea
urchins to clams of all kinds, sea snails to iodine-flavoured *fouskes*
(*violettes*) and for me the most succulent *mezze* of all, the *galypes* or
kolitsanoi, the sea anemone which resembles a cross between an
exotic flower and a jelly fish. This is extracted from the rock with a
fork as it causes irritation to the bare skin when touched; it is then
rinsed well and either dropped in batter and fried or first parboiled

lightly and then mixed with all kinds of chopped wild greens and then fried like rissoles, similar to the *galypokeftethes* of Skyros or Alonnisos.

More importantly, one must not forget that it was from the Aegean islands that fish soups originated, and were taken round the Mediterranean coasts as far as Marseilles, where the local *bouillabaisse* bears a lot of resemblance to the Greek fishermen's soup *kakavia*. *Kakavia* itself can vary a lot. It can be made from the smaller fish in the fishermen's catch, with a little olive oil and perhaps a tomato or two, cooked to a pulp and then sieved. The hard and dried bread that fishermen carry on their boats inevitably finds itself in the soup so that it can soften and become palatable. The islanders, on the other hand, may add the sharp but smooth egg and lemon sauce (the Greek *avgolemono*) to refine their fish soups. A visit to the Greek islands is not complete until a local fish soup has been sampled. You choose a suitable fish such as the ferocious-looking, imperially coloured orange *skorpion* (*skorpina*), a brown *rofos* (grouper), or whatever is on offer at the restaurant. Once it is costed, it is deposited into the cook's hands and miraculously within 30–40 minutes you are served with a uniquely delicious fish soup.

While the culinary theme of the Aegean islands revolves around seafood, in the Ionian one will find surprising influences in the local kitchens which are clearly derived from the islands' past, which is different from that of the Aegean. The Venetian influence is all too evident in the cooking of Corfu with its pasta, veal and rice dishes even if less so in the smaller islands.

Why do the Greek islands hold such fascination though? Is it because these, in some cases bare rocks, have been ravaged and plundered through history by all kinds of conquerors: Phoenicians, Egyptians, Athenians, Macedonians, Romans, Byzantines, Saracens, Venetians, Crusaders, Ottomans, and even Russians for a short period, Italians and lastly the Germans? Or is it that the islanders themselves – passionate and compassionate, hospitable and enthusiastic – have somehow absorbed their environment and their history and thus represent for us our own barely remembered history and mythology? Do we sense in them the compressed qualities of mythical figures? The fascination of mythical Odysseus from Ithaca, the logic of Pythagoras from Samos, the lyricism of Homer from Chios or Sappho from Lesbos?

Enter an island household and you are offered a rush chair under the coolness of the vine, a fruit preserve perfectly balanced on a little spoon accompanied by a cool glass of water; and when the time comes to leave this hospitable scene, the lady of the household will inevitably harvest one or two tender stalks from the perfectly round head of aromatic basil. To these she may add other aromatic items such as silvery, strong-scented *matzourana* or the serrated-leaved *ambarorriza* indispensable for its aroma in spoon preserves (see page 48). She will press the tiny bunch into your hand with emotional wishes to see you again: a wish two thousand years old.

However, if the fruits of the sea account for the main culinary themes of the area, the fruits of the land are similarly treasured, and have been for centuries, since antiquity. One such theme is the use of the fresh, unsalted cheese, the *myzithra*, not only in savoury pies but also in desserts. This is encountered nowadays as it was in the 1880s, when Theodore Bent was travelling round these islands. He remarked,

> Ios is celebrated for its flocks and herds and of all islands Ios is the most celebrated for its myzethra, food for the gods, as they call it. It is simply a curd made of boiled sheep's milk, strained and pressed into a wicker basket called tyrobolon, just as they are spoken of in the 'Odyssey'; from this basket it gets a pretty pattern before being turned out on to a plate. When eaten with honey it is truly delicious.

('THE CYCLADES', J. Theodore Bent, Longmans, Green & Co, London 1885.)

In 1986, when Maroulia Fytrou-Laoutha of Santorini talked about their traditional Easter cakes *militinia*, which are made with the fresh *myzithra*, I asked her where this cheese came from.

BYZANTINE CHURCH, MONEMVASIA

Slightly surprised, she said, 'But from Ios of course!' So much for continuity.

If Greek island life cannot survive without its native seafood, it cannot be conceived of without the ancient silvery presence of the olive trees, withered and wind-blasted at times; or that of their glimmering fruit, the olives and olive oil; or without the satisfying full figures of the huge earthenware jars of Knossos full of this sparkling fruit. These have been present in the Greek islander's life ever since this life was first recorded.

> *The whole Mediterranean – the sculptures, the palms, the gold beads, the bearded heroes, the wine, the ideas, the ships, the moonlight, the winged gorgons, the bronze men, the philosophers – all of it seems to rise in the sour, pungent taste of these black olives between the teeth. A taste older than meat, older than wine. A taste as old as water.*

('PROSPERO'S CELL', Lawrence Durrell, Faber and Faber, London 1975.)

To talk of olive trees, even though fertile Aegean islands such as Mytilini, Samos and Crete are reputed for their olive oil, is to talk of the Ionian Sea; to think of enchanting Corfu with its Italian-influenced dishes and mysterious Ithaca; of pretty Lefkas, idyllic Paxos, capricious Zante and beautiful Kephalonia with its unique pies, some made with meat others with salted cod. Sail round the pointed finger-tips of the Peloponnese with a westerly prow and soon the landscape will be transformed. None of the blue and white interactions of bare Aegean landscapes; the sea here, the Ionian, is pure green, with the landscape reflecting its luxurious lushness into the waters; the beaches are folded in ochre sand rather than the white Aegean pebbles. Then one thinks of cypress trees lazily brushing their caresses against the blue sky, of trees loaded with golden fruit; of corn-flowers and irises, the sweet scent of orange blossom and the wild, thorny roses tumbling over unkempt fences and dry-stone walls. The beautiful Ionian, sophisticated and groomed, subtly sensitive and poetic; a sea of fertile valleys and gardens rather than a sea of white marble; a sea frequented by white doves rather than sharp, daring wild hawks.

But in the lucid twilight that has been encircling us on the warm deck, the soft mauves of an indefinable shape have come into sight, floating towards us. The excitement of the travellers reverberates in the air. The prospect of land, their land, our land. Soon we shall step out onto the promontory rocks, crushing and bruising the low sage bushes on our way. Some distant church bells, from the Prophet Elias church perhaps, as every Aegean island has one, will echo melancholically as in a dream, again and again, enchanted by their own notes, unable to stop. An omen, a good omen. We have arrived. We will find our way up to the *Hora* or *Chorio* and which most Aegean islands exhibit on the brow of a high hill which helped them to keep refuge from fearful pirates and besiegers during their medieval past: Patmos, Alonnisos, Skyros, Serifos, Kalymnos, Amorgos – they all belong to this category.

For it is on these lofty spots that Aegean beauty in all its dazzling splendour unfolds. Stand and gaze at the immense blues encircling you, that of the sea, and sky. Walk through the tiny twisted, stone-flagged village alleys, enter some white and grey pebble-lined courtyard and listen to the Aegean wind whispering at each corner, songs mysterious and enchanted.

We shall describe the journey for you, island by island, rock by rock, but when words are tired perhaps we should leave you with the place itself, as the painter sees it.

Lawrence Durrell wrote in 1946: *The Aegean is still waiting for its painter; waiting in the unselfconscious purity of its lights and contours for someone to go really mad over it with a loaded paintbrush. . . . But to paint Greece one must do more than play with the primary colours; one must convey the soft chalky whiteness of the limestone, the chalk-dust that comes off the columns, the soft pollen-like bloom upon the vases. Then, too, you would have to master the queer putty-mauve and putty-grey tones of the islands – rock that seems to be slowly becoming red-hot. Volcanic notes.* 'Pleasures of New Writing' edited by John Lehman, John Lehman, London 1952.) What we leave you with is an evocation in words and colours.

RENA SALAMAN *Spring 1987*

CYCLADES

*T*his is the dazzling group that embodies the very idea of a Greek island. Every journey around the islands should start here: at charming waterfronts such as Mykonos, enchanted cliffs such as Santorini, with the dazzling whiteness of Paros, the bareness of Ios or Amorgos, the homeliness of Sifnos.

One has not experienced the magic attached to the simple word 'island' until you have sat at the waterfront of these places with an *ouzo* and a few morsels of octopus or with a quartered sugary tomato and just gazed at the setting sun transforming the landscape into a soft mass of colour, as if with a conjurer's wand; or until you have taken a brightly painted blue boat – that unique Aegean blue – and asked the boatman to deliver you to some deserted little bay enclosed by rocks, where armed with the local olives and tomatoes (particularly the little Santorinian tomatoes which taste sweet, like fruit), a small elongated crusty loaf of hot bread, a square slice of white sheep's cheese, some water and a dark green watermelon which you skilfully anchor into the sea to cool, you can spend a blissful day in the blistering heat until your boat returns to collect you in the late afternoon.

SANTORINI

The approach to each island remains an unforgettable experience re-enacted on subsequent visits. The emotions and feelings which well up at first sight of the islands are like those of lovers looking into each other's eyes. These may be of contentment and peace, if the island you approach is like a fertile garden with soft green curves punctuated only by the amorous cypress tops stubbornly piercing the blue sky. Think of Corfu, in the Ionian, Samos or Lesbos in the Aegean. Or it could be love at first sight with the scorched terracotta bareness of any of the Cycladic islands.

The approach to Thera, as it was originally known, or Santorini, the southernmost of the Cycladic islands in the Aegean archipelago, is simply bewitching! The moment the boat sails into the circular blue vacuum of the bay, carefully slipping round the two small volcanic islets in the middle, Palea Kameni and Nea Kameni, there is nothing to match the spell shimmering down from the circular, stripped lava walls towering all around you, in their twisted bareness.

The place reverberates with myth, history and tradition. Have we sailed over the mountain tops into the depths of Atlantis after all? Is this the dream, the myth or the reality?

Some things we know for certain. In 1500 BC the earth shook and burst open with shattering results. The middle of the island, almost half of it, submerged under the primeval force of the sea, to a depth of between 300–400 metres in some parts, while the remaining half was covered with exploding pumice and lava. The tidal wave then rushed southwards on its fatal course, reaching Crete within 30 minutes and annihilating the flourishing Minoan civilization: the coastal settlements of Knossos, Amnissos, Mallia, Phaistos, Paleokastro and the sacred caves were devastated. Luckily Knossos was later rebuilt.

The name Santorini was given to the island by the Crusaders and was derived from a little chapel of Santa-Irini. The island's original name, Thera, was derived from the Lacedaemonian leader, Theras, who founded a settlement on the island, almost a century after the Trojan War. The modern Santorini has a population of six thousand scattered among its thirteen villages.

Today, the white specks of the hilltop villages cling ominously to the clifftop. The capital Fyra and beautiful Oia at the far end look like sparkling stones on a granite crown, frilled with dark beaches made from the blackened, terracotta-coloured pumice pebbles below, or the beautiful black sandy beaches on the south.

A number of unusual specialities figure on a Santorinian table, with the prize going to *domatokeftethes*, a kind of fried rissole made with the local, tiny, uneven, deliciously fruity tomato but no meat.

OIA, SANTORINI

A frugal but mouth-watering combination, surprisingly appetizing. *Fava* (a kind of yellow split pea) is another favourite and Santorinians, a warm, hospitable lot lacking the hawk-eyedness of the Mykonians or Serifiotes for example, proudly believe that their home-grown *fava* is a different affair from that of the rest of Greece. Indeed, it is extremely tasty and sweet.

Santorini is still engulfed in tradition; they still offer *koufeto* at weddings, a kind of caramelized brittle almond concoction offered with the special tiny, two-pronged forks from one platter. (Perhaps this was believed to be an aphrodisiac for the bridegroom. Elsewhere he is given honey with walnuts for the same reason!) Families, having made a wish to a saint, still take over a church devoted to him or her, to have a *panegiri* – a celebration starting with a liturgy which is followed by an enormous feast, consisting of all kinds of salted and dried fish, *domatokeftethes* or anything else they can afford to provide, and wine. Everyone has to be fed, the whole village community including strangers. The merriment and songs resulting from a few glasses of local wine at the church of Aghios Dionysis and the unique welcome that was extended to us at this recent event were monumental proof of the strong traditions of island hospitality.

As a result of the strong traditional character of the island, the cooking remains primarily home-cooking even in the restaurants. One can enjoy the best of seasonal specialities at restaurants such as Karvouni's in Oia, where we were served the most delicious stuffed tomatoes, sprinkled with grated *kefalotyri* cheese, or at the wonderfully old-fashioned, decaying Aktaion at Fyra near the church of Aghios Gerasimos, which also provided the most spectacular sunsets, thrown in, free of charge. And when you descend the 275 or so steps from Oia to the pumice beach of Ammouthi, you can sample as a reward after your climb the cooking of Kyria Katina in her *Iposkafo* restaurant – a typical cave building carved into the cliff. She serves humble but delicious, boiled sweet beetroot with *skorthalia*. This garlic sauce, that has remained a favourite of Greeks since ancient times, has travelled all over the Mediterranean and is found under different guises today and under different names: *tarator* in Turkey, *agliata* in Italy, *Aïoli* in France, *Ali-Oli* in Spain where it has even been transformed into a soup, the Andalousian *gazpacho blanco*. You will also find the baked giant beans or *fasolia gigantes* and of course *domatokeftethes*. All these acquire a Utopian taste after a revitalizing swim in the crystal waters.

One hot, still evening with the huge disc of the moon hanging dangerously overhead, coating the landscape with its golden dust, we took the 20 minutes, walk along the giant cacti-fringed road to Foinikies (Palm Trees) with the vermilion and scarlets of the tangled-fenced bougainvillaeas tumbling down beside us and an exotic scent of the hot red earth permeating the air. We were going there to have dinner at the peaceful, blooming garden of the Foinikies restaurant, with a particular culinary aim in mind: to try the other speciality of the island, *kaparofylla*.

A characteristic *krassomezes* (mezze to be served with wine) from Santorini is made with soaked and boned salted cod, which is then dressed raw with olive oil and lemon and which is locally called *bakaliaros xelouristos*.

Santorini like Monemvasia was famous for its wine:

> *The wine of Santorin keeps a long time, and will stand the longest sea voyages. It pleases the eye with its fine topaz colour, and satisfies the palate with its decided taste; it mixes wonderfully well with water; during two years I drank no other wine at meals. It reminds one a little of Marsala, and has also a slight smack of sulphur; it betrays its origin; grown on a lately extinguished volcano, it is the Lachryma Christi of Greece.*
> *The Russians are very greedy of the Santorin wine; they buy every year fifty thousand drachmas of it; but they would prefer having it for nothing, and to drink it on the spot.*

('GREECE AND THE GREEKS OF THE PRESENT DAY', E. F. V. About, London 1855.)

All in all, Santorini is an island that impresses itself in one's memory, never to be forgotten.

DOMATOKEFTETHES
Tomato Rissoles

What an animated discussion this recipe created in the little courtyard in Oia, where we were all sitting while the explosive sunset of the hot day was busily colouring the capital Fyra across the water and the mountain beyond; so many pinks and mauves and eventually the softest purples, enough to fill a whole colouring book in their own right. (Linda, at the same time, was busily struggling to capture them all, momentary illusions that they are.)

Should one put soda in the mixture? Or soaked stale bread as well as flour as Katina tou Lambrou, who runs the little charming restaurant on the Ammoudi beach below Oia, had told us at lunchtime? After an invigorating swim (to say the least, as the waters are like crystal) that morning, we sampled all her delicacies: sweet beetroot with *skorthalia* (garlic sauce), *fasolia gigantes* (baked giant beans), a tasty relative of the butter bean. Finally, a tomato salad made entirely with home-grown ingredients: the delicious tiny, bright scarlet Santorinian tomatoes, crunchy cucumber which is different from the ordinary cucumber (we used to call this *antzouria* when we were children but which in Santorini they call *katsounia*), the sweetest locally grown onions and of course *domatokeftethes*, the speciality of the island.

One can indulge in the food here as there is no danger of enlarging one's waist, not only because the prime ingredients are so healthy but – and here comes the crunch – because there are 276 handsome steps to climb back to Oia in the dazzling heat. After that you can indulge in another delicious meal in the evening under the starlit sky on the terrace of one of the most unpretentious, unfashionable, but best places in Oia, the Karvounis restaurant. Karvouni's stuffed vegetables with grated *kefalotyri*, served with delicious little crunchy potatoes cut in the *kythonates* style, are the best I have sampled. Well, after my grandmother's that is.

The following day, Maroulia Laoutha, in whose spectacular traditional pension we were staying (practically suspended over the blue sea), announced that she was going to make her *domatokeftethes* specially for us to watch and to sample. For years a friend in Athens had been saying. 'If you go to Santorini make sure you sample Maroulia's *domatokeftethes*.' The day had come and I was thrilled; but first we needed her husband, she said, for the arduous fine chopping of the mound of onions. No, they should not be grated and food processors were an unknown commodity here. Husbands were used instead.

I spotted the loaded donkey meandering down slowly through the little squares as he came down the hillside, disappearing round brilliantly white corners and suddenly Maroulia's husband had arrived; he unloaded the heavy sacks of *fava*, a kind of split pea, from his donkey, and in a little while he had been set on his task in the dark, cool kitchen inside their traditional *iposkafo* building. Maroulia and I made for her a little patch of earth where she harvested her brilliantly scarlet tomatoes while I was given the honorary task of harvesting the mint. She had no basil or parsley as everything had already dried up by early June. Operations were resumed under the vine on the terrace directly in front of her kitchen.

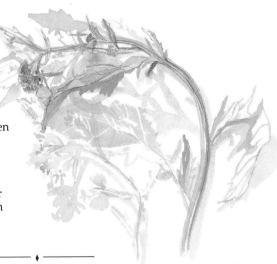

450 g (1 lb) ripe tomatoes, washed and dried
2 medium onions, peeled and finely chopped (not grated)
2.5 ml (½ tsp) paprika
salt and black pepper
90 ml (6 tbsp) fresh mint, finely chopped (about a teacup)

30 ml (2 tbsp) parsley, finely chopped
15 ml (1 tbsp) olive oil
150 g (5 oz/1¼ cups) self-raising (self-rising) flour
sunflower oil for frying

Once she had washed and dried the tomatoes, they were put in a large bowl (for she was making a rather huge quantity in typical Greek fashion) and she squeezed them and manipulated them with her hands, until they had turned into a pulpy substance. This is the only way to do it as you need the skins to give some substance and the tomatoes should not turn into a watery mess. So, no electrical tricks here, but you can chop the onions in a food processor very briefly so that they do not become puréed.

Next mix all the ingredients together, apart from flour; season and mix well. Add enough flour gradually to make a thickish but moist paste. You may not need all the flour. It can wait now until it is time to be eaten.

Put about 2½ cm (1 in) oil in a large frying pan. Heat well but not until smoking and drop in spoonfuls of the mixture. Fry, turning them over until lightly golden all over. Serve immediately as *mezze*.

Serves 4.

MILITINIA
Sweet pastries with Cream Cheese

Among other delicacies peculiar to Santorin is tyropitta, *which literally translated means cheesecake. It is a curious composition, the first ingredient being a curd of sheep's milk (χλωρο), then some eggs, cheese, barley, cinnamon, mastic and saffron. The impression left upon us when tasting it was that it was horrid, but the Santoriniotes are wild about it.*

('THE CYCLADES', J. Theodore Bent, Longmans, Green & Co, London 1885.)

*M*ilitinia are part of the Easter tradition in Santorini and it sounds as if Theodore Bent came upon them a hundred years ago from the above description. No Santorinian household can carry on the ritualistic Easter celebrations without these little sweet pastries.

This is a combined recipe of a num- ber of animated Oian ladies but always with old Nicoletta presiding, firing the instructions in a stern voice. Who would dare disagree with her, since she always added that this was the way her mother used to make them. And her mother according to my calculations must have been of the Theodore Bent era.

---

500 g (1 lb) unsalted cream cheese such as Italian *ricotta* or Cypriot *anari*
500 g (1 lb) caster (superfine) sugar
2 eggs, lightly beaten
50 g (2 oz) plain (all-purpose) flour
40 g (1½ oz) unsalted melted butter
40 g (1½ oz) sesame seeds

500 g (1 lb) fresh or frozen puff pastry, defrosted
1.25 g (¼ tsp) *mastiha* grains, powdered with a little flour to prevent sticking. If you can't find *mastiha* in Greek shops use vanilla essence, although the taste will not be the same

---

Oven: 180°C/350°F/Mark 4.

Beat the lumps out of the chesse with a fork, add the sugar, eggs, flour and *mastiha* and beat well.

Separate the pastry into 2–3 pieces and roll out thinly, one at a time, on a lightly floured surface. Cut rounds 8–10 cm (3–4 in) in diameter, using a small saucer or glass. Place a spoonful of the cheese mixture along the middle of each round and fold over forming a half-moon shape; press the edges together well. Place them on an oiled baking tray and brush their tops with melted butter. Sprinkle a few sesame seeds all over and bake for 35–40 minutes until light golden. Although these taste better when freshly made, they can be kept for a few days, but do not store them in the refrigerator.

Serves 6–8.

KAPAROFYLLA
Salad of Caper Leaves

Everybody in Santorini told us that we should try this sharp appetizing salad which is really more of a mezze and we finally did in the charming garden of the restaurant *Foinikies*.

The method of pickling was explained to me briefly and seemed quite simple. For those of us who may have access to the wild trailing caper plants in some Mediterranean spot, this is what the Santoriniotes do: first gather your leaves (as many as your patience will endure) including whole tops of tender shoots. Wash them and boil them for about 10–15 minutes until almost tender. Strain, discarding the water. Immerse them in cold water for 24 hours. Then strain and immerse in fresh water and leave for 24 hours longer. These steps are taken because, as the locals said, making a very appropriate facial grimace, they are *dilitirio* – bitter, like poison.

Strain, place the caper leaves in an earthenware or glass jar and cover with pure vinegar. When they are to be consumed, take a few out with a slotted spoon, dress them with pure olive oil and sprinkle black pepper on top; absolutely delicious.

Serves 4.

KOUFETO
Bridal Praline

After the religious ceremony was concluded we were all invited to return to the house where in the most limited space possible they danced a syrtos *abominably and administered refreshments – divers kinds of jam, mastic, liqueurs and plates of honey and almond, which last delicacy had to be eaten with a knife.*

('THE CYCLADES', J. Theodore Bent, London 1885.)

This wedding was that of the beautiful daughter of Bent's impoverished muleteer to a small, weedy man who trembled nervously according to the description; but the plates of honey and almond were none other than *koufeto*, which is offered at weddings in Santorini to this day.

Weddings in Santorini are still very traditional and slightly different from other islands. The most striking part of a wedding is when they set off with the priest during the morning of the ceremony to their vineyards where they cut young vine tendrils for making the two crowns required by the Orthodox Church for uniting the couple during the ceremony. Once these have been blessed by the priest on the spot, they are taken home and covered with ribbons and decorated by the bride's friends. Even Theodore Bent was struck by this ritual in the 1880s.

Koufeto is simple to make and it fits the general belief not only here but elsewhere in Greece that walnuts or almonds and honey given to the groom enhance his sexual capability. (No comment.)

Boil 225 g (8 oz) shelled almonds for 2 minutes and skin them; put them in a frying pan and toast them, stirring continuously until aromatic and light golden. Put 225 g (8 oz) honey with 15–30 ml (2–3 tbsp) water in a frying pan or saucepan and heat it gently, stirring to dilute it a little. When hot enough but not boiling, add the almonds, stir to coat them all properly and pour the whole onto a flat platter; let it cool and solidify. It is then offered with special two-pronged forks to all the guests after the wedding ceremony, who break bits of the brittle substance with a special twisting movement of the forks.

Serves 4.

KOLIOI LATHORIGANI
Baked Mackerel with Oregano, Garlic and Lemon

Kyria Maroulia Laoutha talked nostalgically about an old fisherman friend she had some years ago, who would give her the best of his catch for her young children; and would occasionally invite her to join him and the other fishermen at the beach of Armeni near Oia for a *kakavia* (the Greek fishermen's soup). This derives its name from the cauldron-like pot, the *kakavi*, as it was called in ancient Greece.

The fisherman used to imply that she could sample a genuine *kakavia* only when made by a fisherman because, in his exact words, 'you housewives cannot make it properly'. So they would use 2 kg (4½ lb) of their smaller fish for only 3–4 people and would boil them with very little water, a bit of olive oil and an onion, and the result, as one can imagine in such a wonderful setting was absolutely delicious.

Anyway, now that her children are grown up, her son's favourite dish is a *plaki* with small fish such as sardines (*sarthelles*), fresh anchovies (*gavros*), or small mackerel when they can be found in late summer. This is the way she prepares them for him:

4 small mackerel, cleaned but whole
   with their heads on (the smaller they
   are, the tastier and less oily)
salt and black pepper
90 ml (6 tbsp) olive oil
1 lemon

5 ml (1 tsp) dried oregano – the Greek
   rigani
3 cloves garlic, peeled and finely
   chopped
60 ml (4 tbsp) parsley, finely chopped

Oven: 180°C/350°F/Mark 4.

Rinse and season the fish. Arrange them closely, side by side in a small oiled baking dish. Beat olive oil, lemon and seasoning lightly with a fork until well amalgamated. Add remaining ingredients and mix them in; pour this all over the fish and bake for 45 minutes, basting 2–3 times.

Serves 4.

MYKONOS

*Fagame hirokefali, brizola piperati, to skoti tou tiganito, krimas to nio pou
hathi. As tou to tragouthisoume tou hirou to kefali, tou hronou na
xanarthoume na tou to fame pali. As itan ena to krasi kai to yiali potiri kai
stin igia na pinoume tou spitonoikokiri . . .*

(We have eaten the pig's head, sharply peppery chops as well as
his succulent liver, but alas that the young man should go. Let us
sing a song about the pig's head, and let us wish that all being well
we'll gather again next year to eat his head again. Let us fill our
glasses with wine and drink to the health of our host.) This song
was given to me by Mrs Eirene Monoyiou in Mykonos. It conjures
up a pagan Mykonos with her Bacchanalian ancestry. The local
inhabitants worshipped Dionysus and his mother Semeli more
than any of the other gods. These merry, drunken songs are the
traditional accompaniment to the local celebrations at the time of
the slaughter of the family pig in late October, the *hirosfagia*.
Friends and relatives gather to help with the delicate task of
transforming each part of the animal into a succulent mezze, some
for immediate consumption and others to be preserved for the
oncoming winter months. The preserved pieces may be used in
lahana me larthi (casserole of spring greens with salted pork); but
primarily they make the local ham – the well-known *louzes* – which
is pork fillet covered with salt for one night then rinsed and
covered with spices and herbs (allspice, black pepper, rigani,
throubi – a wild aromatic herb of the oregano family) and pressed
into the thick intestine of the animal with one end sewn up; after
that, it hangs in the sun for about a month until it dries out
completely. It can then be hung in a kitchen for up to a year. *Louzes*
are eaten finely sliced, either raw or fried, to accompany a drink.
The locals also make herby sausages, or *syglina* in local dialect,
brawn, salted meat, fried hamburgers (made with the fresh hand-
chopped meat, with onion, soaked bread and rigani). However, to
most of us Mykonos is well known neither for her hams nor her
sausages.

If the mark of the Aegean is the interaction of blue and white, then of all the Aegean islands Mykonos is the pure embodiment of the archipelago. Shadowless and bare with the ripples of her brown earth speckled with the occasional cubic white building and bound by emerald-blue waters, she has an untamed beauty. Do not expect or seek any morsels of kindness in such a beauty for she has all the hallmarks of an uncompromising and opulent sophistication. Aware of her own charms, she will leave you no doubts and no choice. She will cause you to fall in love, and there is no escape, else she may be utterly displeased. She will sweep you off the ground and make you dance through her winding sparkling alleys and imbibe her scents of jasmine, honeysuckle and the hot, faint mustiness of sea-weed.

It is in the early morning that Mykonos displays her beauty at its best; bathed in dazzling light with an unreal definition. Walk at this hour down to the harbour, through the quiet alleys with the narrow external staircases of the houses bursting with colour; with the pinks of trailing carnations, the purples of fuchsias, the scarlet of begonias and the virginal slender lilies, mostly growing out of whitewashed square tins that once housed the *feta* cheese. When you reach the harbour – this is also the best time for all harbours – feast your eyes on the bright colours of the fishing boats coming in to unload their colourful wares by the few marble-topped counters next to the water which make up the fish market of the island. Here are tricycles, loaded with all kinds of eccentric items, some saleable and others not; pots of basil wilting in the sun, baffling home-made cages inhabited by songless crystalline yellow canaries; donkeys a riot of colour with their baskets brimming with freshly cut stocks, carnations and golden marigolds, and the occasional pair of small bright green artichokes sticking out their heads defiantly among the other beauties.

Round the corner, you will be surprised by the happiest sign of everyday life as dark-scarfed ladies return from rock-embroidered gardens beyond the town, with donkeys loaded with produce, not for sale but for the day's meal. Some carry bright purple beetroot,

MYKONOS

the pale young courgettes (zucchini) alongside a small bunch of stocks which will adorn the *saloni* (sitting room) as the table centre-piece. In the old quarter (*kastro*), stand on the promontory of the Byzantine Paraportiani church, which is formed by four different chapels, white walls weaving in and out of white walls, indefinable like a white illusion, and gaze at the blue sea. Invisible behind you, you can sense (though you cannot see) the huge white windmills at the top of the hill at the end of the bay, standing in unison like startled seagulls.

Walk through the tiny alleys from the Paraportiani towards Venezia with the sea breeze blowing in on your right and breathe in the sharp intoxicating sea aroma; and when you reach the famous neighbourhood with the leaning wooden poles resting in the sea supporting decaying, wooden covered balconies, the urge to sit and gaze will be overwhelming. A coffee at this stage is needed. A small revitalizing Greek coffee should be taken in minute sips while you imbibe the atmosphere of Venezia. There are more than 400 chapels in this small town; frugal and simple, most of them have been built by islanders bound by a vow to a saint at a moment of danger at sea. Some are Byzantine, others Roman and all of them pure and simple without the adornments and glitter of the Orthodox Church elsewhere.

On a hot Sunday evening we were invited to a local wedding at the Mitropolis, a small half-sunken church perhaps with more glitter than others on the island. In typical island fashion the instruments at the head of the crowd announced the arrival of the groom and his family with their convivial chirpy noises. Then they turned back immediately to make for the bride's home; some minutes later the violins could be heard again, escorting the young bride all in white with her eyes glimmering in the descending dusk. The little church was bursting at the seams, despite the intense heat, with handfuls of people jostling each other at the doors and windows as well. The priest recited his words through the ceremony at a faster than usual pace until he got to the prescribed moment for handfuls of rice to be thrown at the couple which signify prosperity and fertility in their future life. Everyone breathed a sign of relief as the end of the ceremony came into view and starched white linen squares filled with startlingly white sugared almonds were handed out to each guest, along with little rich chocolate cream pastries wrapped in glittering silver paper. The ceremony was a cross between metropolitan and island tradition but a little different to other traditional island weddings that I had been to.

Mykonos has always been a frugal island; with no land suitable for cultivation her people had to turn to the sea. It was always said that the Mykoniates survived as sailors and pirates. Look at their faces and you can see this past clearly reflected; the sharp refined features, with a pair of sparkling agile eyes, the cosmopolitan spirit of the seafarer combined with the cunning of the pirate – alas turned restaurateur. Their traditional food reflects this fact. Fish of all kinds is baked with garlic and parsley, grilled or made into soups. Octopus and cuttlefish casseroles enrich this trend; but ask any Mykoniati what their most representative dish is and the one closest to their heart and you will get only one answer: *kremmythopitta*. This literally means an onion pie, but in reality more of a cheese pie with onion in it, the most important factor being their own local fresh unsalted cheese called *tyrovolia*, which is mostly made from cow's milk.

Like the rest of the Aegean islands, Mykonos has been conquered and inhabited by various peoples. The Phoenicians, Cretans, Athenians, Spartans and even the Persians landed here on their way back from their defeat at the battle at Marathon. Later the Romans, the Byzantines and in their turn the Venetians, after the fall of Constantinople; Mykonos along with a number of islands at that time was granted to some close relatives of the Doge Dandolo until 1537, when it was taken by El-Din Barbarossa (The Red-Beard), who was dreaded throughout the Aegean. Those who did not escape to nearby Tinos were sold as slaves in eastern markets. Across the water stands Mykonos, twin sister Delos, which has a more glamorous past but not such a glamorous present.

KREMYTHOPITTA
Cheese and Onion Pie

If an island has ever had claims to a specific dish then Mykonos certainly claims this cheese pie (which they, eccentrically, insist on calling an onion pie) as her very own. Although the recipe below is a combination of ideas from various ladies from Mykonos, the pastry is Mrs Kouneni's, who runs the pretty and peaceful Hotel Kouneni near the Mitropolis.

She talked about local food as we sat in the cool of her paved terrace, under the trailing bougainvillaea, at the edge of the beautifully untended, semi-wild orchard.

PASTRY
450 g (1 lb/3¼ cups) plain (all-purpose) flour sifted with a pinch of salt
1 egg
45 ml (3 tbsp) brandy
30 ml (2 tbsp) lemon juice
30 ml (2 tbsp) warm water

FILLING
1 large onion, finely grated
salt and black pepper
500 g (1 lb) *tyrovolia*, fresh unsalted cheese such as the Cypriot *anari* or Italian *ricotta*
60–75 ml (4–5 tbsp) chopped dill
2 eggs, lightly beaten
30 ml (2 tbsp) melted butter

Oven: 180°C/350°F/Mark 4.

Place the sifted flour in a bowl and make a well in the middle; break the egg into the well. Add remaining ingredients and start to mix in the flour, slowly drawing it in a little at a time. When it has all been incorporated, knead the pastry briefly, cover and let it rest at room temperature. Divide the dough into two pieces, one slightly larger than the other. Roll out the larger one quite thinly on a lightly floured surface. Butter a 26 cm (10 in) flan dish (tart pan/pie plate) and line it neatly with the pastry, including its sides. Trim excess edges.

Meanwhile, place the grated onion in a bowl of cold water with 2–3 pinches of salt and leave for 5 minutes. Strain well, squeezing by hand. Place the cheese in a large bowl and add the onion and remaining ingredients apart from the butter and mix well.

Spread the filling evenly over the pastry. Roll out the remaining pastry as thinly as possible and use it to cover the top of the pie. Trim the edges neatly and brush the top liberally with melted butter. Using a small sharp knife, cut the top layer of pastry into oblong or square portions. Cook for one hour.

Serves 6–8.

FASOLIA MYKONIATIKA
Black-eyed Beans with Rice (Mykonos-Style)

*I*n one of the prettiest, dazzling-white alleys in Mykonos overhung with the butterfly-like flowers of the bougainvillaea and balmy with the warm aromas of jasmine and creamy honeysuckle, we couldn't resist stopping and sitting down in the peace of the early morning in June. The winding alley opened into a tiny white-washed square crowned with seven small churches, each devoted to a different saint.

Sitting outside her house, knitting a white cotton lace border, was an elderly lady who talked to us vividly about the square's past history, among other things. Kyria Maroulo Koutsoukou told us about *kremythopitta* (an onion or cheese and onion pie), indigenous to the island, about *kopanisti*, the sharply appetizing creamy cheese made locally either from cow's or sheep's milk. She also talked about black-eyed beans grown locally which made the Mykonian dish *par excellence*, particularly in the past when arid Mykonos knew more frugal days before her sparkling beauty and Daedalian alleys were discovered by tourism.

---

225 g (8 oz) dried black-eyed beans
   (peas)
30 ml (2 tbsp) lemon juice
salt and black pepper
75 g (3 oz/⅓ cup) long-grain rice, rinsed
   and strained

1 large onion, peeled and finely
   chopped
120 ml (8 tbsp) olive oil
2 cloves garlic, peeled and crushed
   (optional)
30 ml (2 tbsp) red wine vinegar

Black-eyed beans do not need soaking and cook in 30 minutes. Sort them to remove grit and stones, wash and strain them. Cover with water, boil for 2 minutes and strain, discarding the water.

Cover the beans with fresh water well above their surface, add the lemon juice (this step will prevent them from discolouring), salt and pepper and cook gently for 20 minutes. Add the rice and more water if needed (it should end up like a thick soup), cover and cook for 10–12 more minutes. Fry the onion in the hot oil in a frying pan until pale golden. Turn the heat down, add the garlic and sauté until just aromatic; add the vinegar, let it bubble for one minute and empty it into the beans; mix and simmer for 5–7 more minutes until the tastes have blended.

This is the kind of dish that calls for the company of sharp black olives and *kopanisti* or sharp *feta* cheese.

Serves 4.

SOUPIES PLAKI
Cuttlefish Casserole with Garlic

My favourite lady in Mykonos is Mrs Taro (Margaritaro) Roussounelou who has the sweetest disposition and the most wonderfully youthful giggle. This recipe is hers. It will make an excellent main course for four, served with a crisp green salad and crusty bread.

1.4 kg (3 lb) cuttlefish, cleaned as
   explained below, washed and strained
150 ml (¼ pint/⅔ cup) olive oil
1 large onion, finely sliced
3 cloves garlic, peeled and halved
juice of half a lemon
225 g (8 oz) fresh tomatoes, peeled,
   seeded and finely chopped

600 ml (1 pint/2⅓ cups) water
700 g (1½ lb) potatoes, peeled, halved
   horizontally and sliced in wedges or
   kythonates as they are called locally
60–75 ml (4–5 tbsp) parsley, washed and
   finely chopped
salt and black pepper

Rinse the cuttlefish first in order to be able to see clearly while cleaning them. Separate the head from the body by pulling it away; cut the body open. Carefully pull out the two silvery ink bags and reserve in a cup as they are indispensable for flavour. Empty the body of all its innards, pull its two wings away, skin it (skinning is not necessary when they are small and people think that the skin adds flavour anyway). Wash and strain. Slice the body into narrow strips about 2.5 cm (1 in) wide and 7.5 cm (3 in) long.

Now deal with the head. Beware not to splash yourself as the upper part, which will be discarded, contains a lot of inky liquid. Discard the round protruding beak first. Cut along horizontally under the eyes, thus separating the tentacles attached on a thin strip (which should be kept) from the upper part which contains the eyes and which should be discarded. Separate the bunch of tentacles into 3–4 small bunches.

Soften the onion gently in the hot oil until glistening. Add the garlic and stir briefly until just aromatic. Turn heat up, add the cuttlefish and fry for about five minutes until all its water has evaporated and it starts to stick. Pour over the lemon juice, tomatoes, salt and pepper, the ink bags if used and half the water. Cover and simmer for 20 minutes. Add the remaining water, potatoes and parsley; adjust seasoning, mix, cover and cook for 30 more minutes, stirring occasionally, until the potatoes are soft.

Serves 4.

SIFNOS

Dazzling white Sifnos is one of the most beautiful islands in the Aegean with a unique gentleness. But when the boat enters its port, Kamares, the visitor might be slightly disappointed. Sifnos' sparkling beauty awaits him inland.

It is in the hilly interior that the traditional beauty of the geometric Cycladean architecture, flanked by the attractive terraced gardens of olive trees, vines, lemon trees and oleanders and dotted by the square shapes of the filigree-ornamented dovecotes, awaits the visitor. The settlement, which includes Artemonas, Pano Petali, its capital Apollònia up on the mountain side with the small villages of Katavati, Exambela and Kato Petali, accounts for the beauty for which Sifnos is so well known. The white of the sparkling houses of the *Hora* is only relieved by the light blue of the church domes and the bright colours of the potted flowers in the village courtyards, the dramatic scarlet of the hibiscus, the soft mottled pinks of carnations, the exotically bright-eyed pelargoniums and the stark reds that are only found in Aegean geraniums; courtyards where the aroma of the basil jostles with the aroma of the *mantzourana* and the *ambarorriza* and the whole with the fragrance of the soft pink lily-like wild caper flowers beside the paths outside. It is not only the houses and churches (there are about 350 on the island) which are whitewashed, but the stone sinks and the contours of the flag stones in alleys and courtyards are also picked out with the white theme, which accounts for the orderly but uniquely satisfying Aegean image. Precious rain water running off the roofs is collected and stored so that their whitewashing also has a practical role in keeping this water clean.

In antiquity, Sifnos was famous for its gold and silver mines and for its potteries. The tradition of pottery is still very strong on the island, but today alas there is no gold or silver in sight. Pretty rusty-coloured pots, plates and cups decorated with attractive creamy or white linear designs are to be found here, reminding one of the connections with the early Aegean themes rather than the elaborate multi-coloured themes of Rhodian or Skyros pottery.

Sifnos is also reputed for its good cooks and a number of her dishes are well known all over Greece, such as *melopitta* (honey-pie), and chickpeas. When talking of chickpeas one is always reminded of the biggest traditional *panegiris* (religious celebration) in Sifnos and of one of the most beautiful monasteries in the Aegean, that of Hrysopigi, where it takes place. The monastery of Hrysopigi, sparkling white, nestles on a rocky projection in the sea and it is connected to the mainland by a narrow little bridge; it is quite close to Apollònia, situated on a lovely little beach with an idyllic decaying taverna beside it. This is where on the 15th August the whole of the island, including its visitors, gather to celebrate the Assumption. When the liturgy is over they all sit down for a communal meal provided by the local families. This meal starts with the *Sifniotika revithia*, the chickpea casserole that has been cooking at the baker's since the previous night and continues with roast lamb, potatoes and plenty of wine. A few cells in the monastery are occasionally offered to visitors, and it is in one of these cells in this most beautiful and mystical of settings that the Sifnian poet Aristomenis Provelengios wrote most of his poems, years ago.

And for our last stop, we visit Kastro, the old capital of the island from antiquity until the 19th century; Kastro (castle), as its name suggests, was a defensive settlement on the top of a hill, with rows of dense housing forming its outer wall. A number of shields of the noble houses and churches built inside the Kastro during the 17th and 18th centuries can still be seen and the whole semi-deserted place is permeated with mediaeval melancholy and vibrates with enchantment; it is the most suitable place to say farewell to the beauty that sparkles under the sun in the middle of the archipelago, Sifnos.

REVITHIA SIFNOU
Sifnian Chickpea Casserole

Chickpeas always bring Sifnos to my mind. The dish which is most commonly associated with the beautiful island is a chickpea casserole which is usually taken to the local baker on a Saturday night, or at any rate on the night before it is to be eaten, where it cooks in a slow oven all night. The water the baker uses is rain water, which is why the finished dish tastes so delicious. The baker seals the rim round the cover of the casserole with bread dough so that no flavour escapes and by the next morning the chickpeas have been transformed into a thick, soft and delicious concoction.

As Sifnos is also well known for her attractive traditional pottery there is a special terracotta-coloured pot for this dish, which is called *skepastaria*.

350 g (12 oz) chickpeas, picked over and
    soaked overnight
1 large onion, peeled and finely sliced
2 cloves garlic, peeled and finely sliced
150 ml (¼ pint/⅔ cup) olive oil

1 bay leaf
15 ml (1 tbsp) plain (all-purpose) flour
    diluted in a little cold water
salt and black pepper
lemon quarters to garnish

Oven: 150°C/300°F/Mark 2.

Rinse and drain the chickpeas. Place them in a large saucepan, cover with cold water. Boil for 2 minutes and strain, discarding the water.

Place the chickpeas in an ovenproof casserole, preferably earthenware, with remaining ingredients and enough water to reach 10 cm (4 in) above their surface; mix well, cover first with foil and then put the lid on top and cook overnight in a very slow oven. The next morning they will be a delicious soft mass.

Serves 4–6.

MELOPITTA SIFNOU
Honey Pie from Sifnos

A kind of cheesecake but with the unmistakable aroma of honey. The best alternative to the creamy unsalted Aegean cheese is the Italian *ricotta* or Greek Cypriot *anari*. However, I have made it with equal amounts of cottage cheese and ordinary cream cheese and the result was still good.

PASTRY
200 g (7 oz/1½ cups) plain (all-purpose) flour, sifted with a pinch of salt
100 g (4 oz/1 stick) butter
45 ml (3 tbsp) cold water

FILLING
450 g (1 lb) creamy Italian *ricotta* cheese (or see above)
75 g (3 oz/6 tbsp) caster (superfine) sugar
3 eggs, beaten
15 ml (1 tbsp) plain (all-purpose) flour
60 ml (4 tbsp) aromatic clear honey
2.5 ml (½ tsp) cinnamon

Oven: 180°C/350°F/Mark 4.

Rub the butter into the flour to the consistency of breadcrumbs. Add the water and make a shortcrust pastry; this can be made successfully in a food processor. Let the pastry rest a little and then roll it out thinly on a lightly floured surface and line the base of a round 23–26 cm (9–10 in) tart dish (pan).

Mix the cheese and sugar together well. Beat the eggs with the flour and add to the cheese; add the honey and half the cinnamon and work thoroughly, until properly incorporated. Spread evenly on top of the pastry and cook for 45 minutes until light golden; take out and sprinkle the remaining cinnamon all over the top while hot.

Serves 6.

LOUKOUMATHES
Crisp Honeyed Doughnuts

*An old man prepared us a capital meal of fish and light cakes with honey
poured over and told us much about the visit of King Otho and
Queen Amalia.*

('THE CYCLADES', J. Theodore Bent, Longmans, Green & Co,
London, 1885).

*L*oukoumathes are traditionally made in the Aegean islands when the foundations of a new house (the *themelia*) are laid; or for baptisms. At weddings they are offered on large platters to bystanders as the bride in her plumage and her groom open the traditional *syrto* dancing in the village square.

---

225 g (8 oz/1¾ cups) plain (all-purpose)
  flour
large pinch salt
6 g (¼ oz) sachet easy blend dried yeast
  or 15 g (½ oz) fresh yeast
240 ml (8 fl oz/1 cup) warm water

2.5 ml (½ tsp) sugar if fresh yeast is used
300 ml (½ pt/1⅓ cups) or more sunflower
  oil for deep frying
35–40 ml (7–8 tsp) aromatic clear honey
5 ml (1 tsp) cinnamon

Sift flour and salt in a bowl and mix with the dried yeast; add the warm water, slowly beating at the same time. Beat for about 2–3 minutes until the mixture looks smooth and lightly frothy. Cover with a kitchen towel and let the mixture rest in a warm place for one hour, until it has doubled in size.

If using fresh yeast, dissolve the yeast in about 60 ml (4 tbsp/¼ cup) of the warm water, add the sugar to activate it and let it stand in a warm place for about 15 minutes, until it starts to froth. Empty it into the middle of the sifted flour, beating all the time. Add the remaining water, and beat until the mixture becomes smooth. Cover with a tea towel and leave in a warm place for about 2 hours until doubled in size.

Heat the oil in a deep fryer or a saucepan; drop 75–90 ml (5–6 tsp) of the mixture into it at a time, dipping the spoon into cold water between additions to keep the dough from sticking. Each drop will puff up and rise to the surface within seconds. Cook for about 1½ minutes, turning them over from time to time. As they become pale golden, lift them out with a slotted spoon and drain on absorbent paper.

Serve 4–5 for each person on a small flat plate, dribble a spoonful of honey all over. Sprinkle some cinnamon over the top and serve immediately.

Makes about 30.

SYROS

The traditional island of Syros is the capital of the Cyclades and only four hours away from Pireans. My childhood impression of Syros was not of a holiday island, unlike her neighbours, but as an important place of commerce, tradition and wealth. She has kept this image, if not her position, nowadays, among the Aegean islands. Syros has been known for its cultural heritage, as becomes a capital, her seafaring tradition, her captains, her ship-building and . . . her *loukoumia* (Turkish delight). Hermoupolis the main town and port, is named after Hermes the god of trade and commerce, and bears the marks of a prosperous city: beautiful neo-classical houses and a Town Hall; a beautiful theatre built to resemble La Scala in Milan and the Customs House built by the German architect Ziller; public squares filled with flowers and adorned by palm trees; the elegant large houses of the seafaring families with their heavy ornate gates, their charming balconies proudly facing the elements and the blue expanse of the sea.

Along the waterfront and around the main square, Miaouli, tavernas and *ouzeri* offer a selection of homely cooking – all exuding the aroma of the sun-dried octopus being grilled over charcoal. Sample the Syriani courgette (zucchini) pie, the cheese pies or courgettes stuffed with cheese and immersed in a sharp egg and lemon sauce; or the freshly caught silvery *melanouria* (sea bream), served with a caper sauce (or *maintanosalata*), a kind of local esoteric *skorthalia* (a garlic sauce, page 61). Don't miss a walk round the small neighbourhood of Vrondatho with its small and simple houses, where the low-ceilinged, unpretentious little tavernas and *ouzeri* that the fishermen and sailors frequent are to be found.

Journey inland to spots like Mana (Mother) and Possidonia, which with their almond trees, pine- and palm-fringed gardens are like little oases compared to the rest of the island.

KOLOKYTHOPITTA
Courgette (Zucchini) Pie

*L*ike the rest of the Greek islands, Syros has a fondness for pies, which despite their simple ingredients make delicious meals and have a *decorum* that makes them fit for special occasions.

90 ml (6 tbsp) olive oil
1 large onion, finely sliced
3 spring onions, finely sliced
700 g (1½ lb) courgettes (zucchini), trimmed, washed and scraped lightly
75 g (3 oz/⅓ cup) long-grain rice, rinsed and strained
100 g (4 oz) *feta* cheese or Caerphilly, crumbled
75 ml (5 tbsp) milk
4 eggs, lightly beaten
3 tbsp each of chopped fresh dill or mint and parsley
salt and black pepper
PASTRY
1 packet *fyllo* pastry
150 g (5 oz/1¼ sticks) butter, melted

Oven: 180°C/350°/Mark 4.

Heat 75 ml (5 tbsp) of the olive oil and sauté the onions. Grate the courgettes coarsely and mix with the onions and other filling ingredients.

Use a medium-sized roasting dish (pan). Trim the pastry, allowing at least 10 cm (4 in) for shrinkage at either end. Oil the dish (pan) with the remaining olive oil and line its base with a sheet of pastry that has been brushed with butter first. Continue in the same fashion, brushing each sheet with butter first, until half the pastry has been used. Spread out the filling evenly and fold all the pastry sides over it. Cover with the remaining pastry, brushing each sheet with butter first. Trim the excess all round or tack them in at the sides.

Using a sharp knife cut the top layers of pastry only (otherwise the filling might spill) into square or lozenge pieces, approximately 5×8 cm (2½× 3 in). Sprinkle a little cold water with the tips of your fingers to prevent the *fyllo* edges curling up.

Bake for one hour, until crisp and light golden.

Serves 6.

TARAMOSALATA
Taramosalata

Lent in all its earnest asperity was now in full swing; we knew that in the interior no flesh could be obtained, so we purchased another fat lamb to take with us. Lent is indeed a fearful season of abstinence. Like the nuns of Tenos, we found many women performing the trimeron *or three days' fast, on nothing but water and for the first week the truly pious would not think of touching anything but vegetables and bread. If an animal falls ill during this long fast they kill it and pickle it for the Easter feast; every egg that a hen lays during this period is hard-boiled and put by till the fast is over; so to guard against starvation we took with us our lamb and a little caviare, which came in most opportunely.*

('THE CYCLADES', J. Theodore Bent, Longmans, Green & Co, London 1885.)

This was the situation Bent encountered during the Greek *Sarakosti* (Lent) on the island of Andros. The situation is not that different nowadays although one would not have to take 'a fat lamb'. However, the menu would be frugal and would probably consist of lentil or bean soup. But one thing you would certainly find in every household and in almost every restaurant is *taramosalata*, which enlivens the Lenten table. It is made from *tarama* the salted and dried roes of large fish such as cod or grey mullet. You can substitute the fresh, smoked cod's roe, particularly the undyed variety which is a dull orange colour.

---

100 g (4 oz) crustless stale bread
175 g (6 oz) fresh smoked cod's roe or
   75 g (3 oz) salted Tarama
juice of 1½ lemons

90 ml (6 tbsp) olive oil
1 thin slice of onion (optional)
a few black olives to garnish

Soak the bread in water for 10 minutes. Squeeze it a little but leave it still a little moist. Put it in a food processor or blender. Skin the fresh roe and add it to the bread with the lemon juice and the onion. Blend until smooth and start adding the oil slowly while the blades are in motion. If it is too stiff at this stage, add 5–10 ml (1–2 tsp) of cold water. Blend, taste and adjust accordingly. If a milder taste is preferred, add a little more bread and oil. Serve on a plate dotted with the olives.

Serves 4.

NERANTZI GLYKO
Bitter Orange Spoon Preserve

To his wife Kyria Matzi we shall be for ever grateful, for immediately on our arrival she introduced us to the great Andriote luxury limonakki, *tiny green lemons made into a jam so deliciously soft and so deliciously sweet that we longed for a potful and some bread and butter.*

('THE CYCLATHES', J. Theodore Bent, Longmans, Green & Co, 1885.)

The custom is no different now. The visitor will still be regaled, at any island household, with treasured spoon preserves of aubergines, morello cherries, rose petals and pistachios.

---

1 kg (2 lb) Seville oranges (about 8 oranges)
1 kg (2 lb/5 cups) caster (superfine) sugar

150 ml (¼ pint/⅔ cup) water
juice of half a lemon

Wash and dry the oranges. Grate them lightly and discard the zest, which can make the preserve bitter. Slice each one into four pieces vertically or into six if large. Discard the flesh and drop the pieces of peel into a bowl of cold water. Have a tapestry needle with a double thread ready. Roll each piece lengthways and thread it. Once you have threaded about 10 pieces, tie the two ends securely, forming a little necklace. You will end up with 3 such necklaces. Rinse and immerse them in fresh cold water for 24 hours, changing the water 3–4 times.

Place them in a saucepan with 2.8 litres (5 pints/2½ quarts) of fresh water. Boil half-covered for 15 minutes and strain, discarding the water. Cover with the same amount of fresh water and simmer about 10 minutes until tender. (Try piercing one with a toothpick.) Strain and leave for one hour.

Mix the sugar and water in a large saucepan over gentle heat, stirring continuously. Once the sugar is dissolved, boil gently for about 4 minutes until it bubbles and thickens and starts to set. Cut the threads and add the pieces to the sugar; cook for five minutes. Remove from the heat and leave overnight or for 5–6 hours.

Bring back to the boil and boil gently for 4–5 minutes uncovered until thick and starting to set. (Bear in mind that it will set further as it cools down so do not cook further.) Add the lemon juice, remove from heat, let it cool completely and pack into sterilized jars.

Offer a piece on a spoon, resting in a saucer, along with a glass of water.

Makes 30–32 pieces.

THE HARBOUR, SKOPELOS

SPORADES

This is a group with an identifiable beauty all to itself. Predominantly it is its lushness and its emerald seas that create the overall impression, distinct from the bareness of the Cyclades or the Dodecanese.

Skiathos is beautiful with its picturesque whitewashed town and its dazzling white sandy beach, *Koukounaries*, one of the best beaches in Greece. As the boat turns suddenly to the right into the main harbour of Skopelos, the visitor will be astounded by one of the most beautiful traditional towns in Greece built round the mulberry-studded harbour. Walk around its winding streets in the early hours of the morning before the heat sets in, peep behind windows curtained with the starched whiteness of hand-made lace and absorb the thousand details that comprise her unique traditional character; watch the local women cleaning their already sparkling clean courtyards brimming with potted plants behind decorative iron railings, or peel the day's vegetables sitting at their front steps, and breathe in the various cooking smells emerging irresistibly from the kitchens; take a look into the colourful containers waiting to be baked at the local bakers, at the local shopkeepers sleepily opening their accordion-like shutters, at, here, a wonderfully old-fashioned barber with a fabulous gilded mirror or, there, a whitewashed butcher's shop, empty of carcasses at this early hour. When you reach the Ioannis Gikas baker's shop, behind the Post Office, you must go in and get a couple of boxes of the freshest honey-dripping *baklavathes* and the wonderfully moist *karythopitta* (walnut pie) and immerse yourself in the baking aromas, a unique mixture of vanilla and cinnamon; this is the place that supplies all the *zaharoplastia* (sweet pastry shops) at the waterfront, so not only are you buying the best but also the cheapest.

At lunchtime, walk to the opposite end of the harbour and eat at one of the two best restaurants in town, the Klimataria next to the

Municipal building or at Angelos at the far end. Taste the wonderful *katsikaki giouvetsi* (kid baked with pasta and fresh tomatoes), or a vivid pink snapper (*lithrini*) with charcoal marks. Or take the rickety bus and drive through plane-studded countryside to the beautiful sandy beach of *Staphylos* or the enchanting bay of *Agnontas* on the opposite side of the island and the sleepy village of *Glossa* with its red-tiled roofs punctuating the green of the hillsides.

The specialities are common to the group: the special *taramokeftethes* (rissoles made from salted fish roe, wild greenery collected from the hills and breadcrumbs), *kolokythokeftethes* (courgette rissoles), the multitude of pies and the seafood. One should try the *galypokeftethes* (a sea anemone resembling a small jelly fish, which is poached and then fried in batter for the most eccentric but succulent of seafoods), which is particularly good on Skyros. Frugal *fava*, a kind of split pea, is particularly good on Skyros with the added aroma of the wild fennel sprigs scattered with olive oil, onion and lemon juice all over its top.

However, we have not talked yet of Alonnisos and its charms; the generosity and simplicity of its people: our friends who deposit freshly gathered fruit, or a bottle of dark green olive oil, or a bowl of freshly made *xynogalo* (sour cheese), on our table in the garden early in the morning without being seen, our friend Barba-Nikos, dark and thin like a reed with one unique tooth in his mouth, who arrives after singing in the church on Sundays loaded with purple figs or the biggest bunches of *rigani* (wild oregano) and *thymari* (thyme) that one has even seen. He is the stone-mason, building beautifully laced walls out of ordinary stones; a summer without him is inconceivable and when we run out of stone walls to build, we demolish some and start again. After lunch, when one or two cold beers have been consumed and once the winter gossip has been exhausted, his unique, wailing voice rises in some of the old bridal songs of the island, and is complemented by the lively cicadas. There is more on Alonnisos, as she is, to me, more like home than Athens is nowadays and her beauty keeps me going on dark winter days.

ALONNISOS

When the little boat called *Kyknos* (Swan) turned left into the perfectly circular harbour during a hot afternoon in the middle sixties, my eyes filled with magic and I was overwhelmingly aware that this was a significant arrival. One could not wish for a more naturally beautiful harbour; the embodiment of an idyll. In the blinding sun, the bay glittered like a bright disc. Sleepy and deserted in her afternoon slumber, Alonnisos lay in repose like a paradise as yet undiscovered.

Alonnisos with her generous curves softly filled with domesticated fauna in the west and with wild undergrowth on her mountainous east: silver olive trees, the young green of almond trees, walnut, quince and peach trees, ilex, glossy arbutus, bay bushes, thyme, balmy sage, and pine trees. In springtime these hills are transformed like the huge palette of a painter whose bright colours have spilled into one another and painted the huge yellow patches of daisies, the bold scarlet of poppies, the mauves of the cornflowers. You cannot help thinking that these are the colours under which paradise must have been conceived as a poetic idea.

In the far distance the highest of the hills can be seen crowned by the white specks of village houses dribbling down the hillside; Alonnisos proper: the original eponymous 13th-century village, built away from the sea and walled against pirates and wandering Saracens. It is from this top that beauty can be experienced in all its splendour; and the result is overwhelming.

Sit on the bullet-studded stone wall under the two mulberry trees on a late afternoon, in the eccentrically named *Kopria* (the manure), which is the main village square, but looks more like a stage against the horizon. Gaze at the blazing disc of the sun coated in gold dust, turning into fire as the evening proceeds until it descends at a fast pace, rests and disappears below the horizon at sea level – a ball of fire. Here are none of the soft pinks and gentle purples of the Cyclades, of Santorini or of Mykonos; this is grand, spectacular and forceful.

When the sun is down and in the interval before the sky fills with sparkling stars, ask Nina who owns the original taverna in the village, just up the 4–5 steps from you, to make you one of her crisp exquisite local *tyropittes* (cheese pies). She won't always succumb, but if you are lucky and get her in the right mood (the people up here are wild like their setting sun), she may even let you watch her, while she dextrously rolls out a sheet of pastry like the perfect circle of the finest of gauze, with her long, thin elegant rolling pin.

For some Alonnisians, the view from the square was the last thing they ever saw. The square was chosen by the Germans not for its grand views but for a *tour de force* on the afternoon of the 15th August 1944. Having gathered together the whole village with the help of Greek collaborators, they picked 14 men accused of leftist tendencies and executed 13 of them, hence the bullet-ridden wall. The remaining survivor, Apostolis Vlaikos, now rather elderly but still charming, is our island bank manager. He was spared, and instead his wife and their first baby, only hours old, were dragged from their house which was then burnt.

Kopria may be the best spot at sunset, but, in the morning, sit under the thatched roof of Panayiotis Kaloyiannis' taverna, *Aloni* (the threshing stone), at the edge of the village and know what it is to be a bird, floating high above sea and land. Gaze towards the two little stony islands, Stavros (the cross, which it literally resembles) and Manola. While you are there do not miss their wonderful *avga matia* (fresh fried eggs) accompanied by a small white cup of steaming Greek coffee. Or sit here in the late afternoon with a cloudy thimbleful of *ouzo* and enjoy a gentle and peaceful spectacle while the invisible sun behind you obstructed by a hill throws its suffused light onto the little islands. For some of the best cooking in the old village visit the Malamatenios taverna next door to Aloni, which, although it lacks the views, will reward you with some of the best local dishes. For instance, try their baked sword fish with potatoes and lemon, or their giant beans (*fasolia gigantes*), their cheese pies, their stuffed vegetables and, in the spring, the pies filled with wild greenery.

From here one can walk down to the beach of *Megalo Mourtia* through the pine trees and tangled undergrowth; there you will be rewarded not only by the beautiful dense olive groves bordering the beach but by two of the best tavernas on the island, the Meltemi and the Mourtias. Both are run by local families who have owned the piece of land for generations, and the cooking is done by the respective matriarchs. The food, as you may have guessed, is exquisite; it would make the best possible introduction to Greek food.

Take the little boats that leave Patitiri harbour every morning and visit one of the beaches on the east of the island, such as Chrisi

PANAYIOTIS KALOYIANNIS' TAVERNA, OLD ALONNISOS

Milia, Georgi Yialo or Ais Petros, where Nina Maniou makes the best stuffed courgette flowers and the most exquisitely crisp version of cheese pie. If during your stay you are lucky enough to have a full moon on one of those nights that the world seems to stand still and the surface of the sea is dappled with silver dust, take an evening trip to the furthest-away village of Kalamakia, about an hour away from Patitiri. Most probably your evening will be animated by the chirpy violin playing of the owner of the local taverna and the perfect circle of the Greek dancers will be off. When your boat turns its prow towards home, quite merry by then with *retsina*, you will probably surrender to the beguiling mysteries of the moonlit night and murmur a new tune to accompany the soft, monotonous pat-pat of the engine.

TONNOS PLAKI
Baked Tuna

Early in September the tuna season starts and all the locals can talk about nothing else as they eagerly await the return of the fishing boats with the first of the catch. Tuna is then fried and served with or without *skorthalia* (garlic sauce). However, their favourite way is to bake tuna as described here in Maria Karakatsani's recipe.

1 medium onion, finely sliced
2 cloves garlic, peeled and finely sliced
75 ml (5 tbsp) olive oil
2 large tomatoes about 275 g (10 oz),
    peeled, seeded and chopped or grated

salt and black pepper
60 ml (4 tbsp) finely chopped parsley
4–5 tuna steaks
30 ml (2 tbsp) olive oil

Oven: 180°C/350°F/Mark 4.
Brown the onion and garlic lightly in the hot oil. Add the tomatoes and seasoning and cook for 10 minutes. Mix in the parsley. Oil a medium roasting tin, lay the fish in it in one layer, sprinkle over some seasoning and spread a tablespoon of the sauce over each slice of fish. Pour in 75–90 ml (5–6 tbsp) water and sprinkle the remaining olive oil all over the top.
Bake for 40 minutes.

Serves 4.

TYROPITTA ALONNISIOTIKI
Alonnisian Cheese Pie

These absolutely delicious cheese pies are the speciality of Alonnisos and Skopelos. Island women make pastry most dextrously and the thinness of the pastry accounts for the charm of these pies. The other crucial factor is that they should be consumed as they emerge crisp and hot from the oil of the frying pan.

There is nothing better for a hot lunch under an olive tree, and children adore these *tyropittes*. They are circular and flat, coiled in snail-like fashion with *feta* cheese nestling inside their folds. They measure about 20 cm (8 in) in diameter and one of them is enough for two people with a tomato salad.

The women of Alonnisos pride themselves on their *tyropitta*-making and it is a delight to watch their hands

flying over the huge round wooden board they use, manipulating their long, thin and elegant rolling pin, resulting in the most perfect circular and paper-thin pastry; then they crumble their white cheese all over it with the tips of their fingers, folding it with light and artistic movements which are extremely satisfying to the eye.

Tyropittes are consumed in Alonnisian homes for lunch or dinner as they are quite substantial and the women will always make one or two extra ones for the man of the household to take to the fields, the olive groves, or the pine forests up, towards Gerakas, where the men go at dawn to extract the *retsini* – the pine resin which tumbles like tear drops down the tree trunk into little corroded tin cups.

---

225 g (8 oz/1¾ cups) plain (all-purpose) flour
pinch of salt
75–90 ml (5–6 tbsp) cold water

FILLING
200 g (7 oz) *feta* cheese, crumbled
30 ml (2 tbsp) olive oil
Olive oil for frying

Sift flour and salt together. Make a well in the middle, add the water and gradually mix it in with the flour, making quite a firm dough. Gather into a ball, dust with flour and knead it hard, folding it over until it feels quite elastic. Cover with a cloth and let it rest at room temperature for at least 30 minutes. Divide into two; roll one out at a time, dusting with flour as necessary, into a large circular disc

about 45 cm (18 in) in diameter. Dribble the olive oil in circles all around its surface, and crumble all over the rather dry *feta*. (If the cheese is wet it should be drained first.)

Roll the half of the circle lying in front of you like a cigar, towards the middle where hypothetically its diameter should lie; then taking the opposite side, do the same, in such a fashion that the two edges are lying parallel and do not overlap. Take one of the two ends and curl it inwards, horizontally; then curl the other end round this, until the strip has been coiled like a snail. Slip your palm underneath it carefully. Lift it and place it on a flat plate. Heat the oil in a frying pan, then slide the pie off the plate into the hot oil. Fry over a medium heat for 2–3 minutes, lift with a spatula and turn over carefully; fry for 2–3 more minutes or until it looks crisp and light golden. If you don't like too much oil, drain it on absorbent paper for a few minutes. Eat immediately.

Makes 2 tyropittes.

IMAM BAYILDI
Baked Aubergines (Eggplant) with Tomatoes and Garlic

After a hot 20-minute walk through a pine forest we descend to the blazing blue beach of Megalo Mourtia. In the summer, every Tuesday and Friday the local broad-bodied caique arrives at dawn loaded with all the provisions needed by the island – among other things, brightly coloured vegetables and fruit, and bunches of fresh greens from the city of Volos on the mainland. On those days delicious vegetable dishes such as *briami*, okra casseroles, *moussaka* and my favourite *imam* figure in most of the restaurants.

Imam, one of the best aubergine dishes, is the speciality of Kyria Maria Karakatsani, the matriarch who presides over the kitchen of the charming family restaurant *Meltemi*, down by the white-pebbled beach.

She always reserves some *imam* for me because she knows my passion for it, particularly when it is accompanied by a plate of bright green boiled *vlita* from their garden. Quite often her husband, Mitsos Karakatsanis, gives us a bundle of newspaper sheets full of the young shoots of wild *glystritha* (purslane) which grows like a weed in his garden. Once chopped and dressed with their fragrant olive oil and lemon this makes the crunchiest, most appetizing and most refreshing of salads. He always brings us some fruit as it ripens on his trees: pink cherries, the sweetest little apricots, or some light green plums, the early green figs which are called *apostoliatika* or the local small juicy peaches. The tables placed in the olive grove under the shade of the huge, dense olive trees are the most simple and idyllic setting for a restaurant. When such a setting is blessed with the exquisite cooking supplied by both beach restaurants (for Kyria Angeliki of the restaurant at the edge of the olive grove is also an excellent cook), then this is indisputably one of the most desirable beaches in the Aegean.

Occasionally our friend Petros, who is an obsessive and devoted spear-gun fisherman, returns in the late afternoon with a substantial catch, perhaps a thick ugly-looking, yellow-spotted *smerna* (moray-eel) or some flat glistening silver *skatharia* or *melanouria* (sea bream). Then the decision is taken to stay and have the fish cooked on the beach for supper. The restaurant, which normally closes at dusk, remains open and Kyria Maria is set on the task of frying the deliciously rich-tasting pieces of *smerna*, or making a casserole of *octopus stifatho*, if the creatures were unfortunate enough to cross Petros' path. Rapidly, the sun is turning golden in its westerly path over the floating rocky image of Skopelos across the water, painting it with the softest colours which only a sunset knows how to, the mauves, the pinks, the purples, and finally when the sun has set beyond Skopelos, an iridescent silvery gleam is dusted over the still waters. The beach is deserted, the shadows in the still olive grove

VIEW FROM RENA'S HOUSE, OLD ALONNISOS

lengthen, the air is fragrant with the aromas of thyme and sage; enchantment is in the air and thousand-year-old spirits are about. This is the most complete, beautiful and mystifying moment of the day.

Then we all settle around a long trestle table, including the whole Karakatsanis family and feast and drink while the children play a game of hide-and-seek, hiding like swallows up the olive trees or behind the dry stone walls. Others collect limpets off the rocks on the beach, or frighten each other with ghostly stories about the floating *smerna* head while the most daring ones try to catch an octopus by

waving a white cloth in front of what they imagine to be his nest. By now, old Mitsos' spirits are quite high (even by local standards) and with eyes glistening like coals he starts singing exquisite wailing verses of island songs with his voice palpitating with passion. Now, he is in the prime of his youth, the civil war, the Albanian mountains, hiding around the island from the German forces, it is all there, resounding with a precise echo from the opposite hillside under the olive trees. And as a pale and shy quarter-moon rises and fills with colour we start our, ascent to the old village. Tomorrow is another lovely day!

———— ♦ ————

4 slim aubergines (eggplants) about 1 kg (2 lb)
275 g (10 oz) onions, finely sliced
150 ml (¼ pint/⅔ cup) vegetable oil, for frying aubergines
4 cloves garlic, finely sliced
60 ml (4 tbsp) olive oil

500 g (1 lb) tomatoes, peeled and chopped, or a 396 g (14 oz) tin (can)
5 ml (1 tsp) dried oregano
1.25 ml (¼ tsp) dried thyme
60 ml (4 tbsp) parsley, finely chopped
5 ml (1 tsp) tomato purée (paste) diluted in a teacup of hot water
salt and black pepper

———— ♦ ————

Oven: 180°C/350°F/Mark 4.

Leave the aubergines whole with their stalks on, wash and dry them. Slit them carefully lengthwise on one side only, like a pouch. Fry them whole, turning them over until light golden. Arrange them side by side in a medium-sized oven dish and season.

In the meantime, sauté the onions in the olive oil until they start to become lightly coloured. Add the garlic and stir briefly until aromatic; add the fresh

tomatoes, herbs and seasoning and cook for 15 minutes. (If using a tin, chop the tomatoes but keep most of the juice aside.)

Fill the half-slit aubergines with this mixture. Add the reserved tomato juice to the pan or if fresh tomatoes have been used, the diluted tomato purée. Bake for 50 minutes, basting occasionally.

Serves 4.

NORTH AEGEAN ISLANDS

*I*f the Cyclades represent the startling temptress outstretched in the middle of the archipelago, a little further North there lies the pretty but sedate and orderly daughter of the sea: the North Aegean islands.

The group includes beauties such as Samos (birthplace of Pythagoras and Epikouros), with its wooded slopes which seem to be frequented by Fauns and Nereids, and its enhancing silky beaches. Samos has been reputed for its sweet wines. My first introduction to them was at church when as a child I had to fast for a couple of days and then have the Greek Orthodox Communion. This consisted of a spoonful of a ruby-coloured, warm, richly sweet and scented wine which in the early morning had a miraculous effect on my empty and previously fasting stomach, to say the least! It sent me back home dancing all the way! A little further north, Chios, home of the mastic tree, from which the strong drink called *mastiha* is made. Visit the village of Pyrgi with its large and elegant houses, beautifully and uniquely decorated with geometric designs. Chios also claims to be the birthplace of Homer.

Luscious Mytilini or Lesbos, home of the poetess Sappho. Also famed for its wonderful olive oil and the *ouzo* from the charming village of Plomari. One of the prettiest and most colourful villages in the Aegean, the fishing village of Molyvos is perched on the north-west tip of the island.

And last comes rocky Limnos whose deep bright blue waters abound in fish and lobsters. On flights to the island from Athens, we used to place our orders over the radio, so that on arrival there would be strings of rosy *Barbounia* (red mullet), exquisitely fresh prawns and wonderful eggs for the crew to take back to Athens.

DOLMATHAKIA
Stuffed Vine Leaves

*T*here cannot be Lent in Greece without the green presence of stuffed vine leaves, with all the aromas of the Greek hillsides, just like there cannot be a garden without the overhanging *klimataria* (vine) providing its eternal shade.

Appropriately called *dolmathakia sarakostiana* (Lenten stuffed vine leaves), they are the favourite of frugal Greek islanders, not only during Lent but also throughout the summer months. These Lenten *dolmathakia* do not contain meat and their appealing charm relies heavily on the quality of the fragrant olive oil, the aroma of slender *maratho* (fennel), which can be found nestling in the moist shade of the twisted fig trees on the hillsides, or the fragile wild mint and most importantly on the unmatched refreshing taste of the fresh, young vine leaves.

As the green island of Lesbos, virtually choked with the silvery presence of the olive trees, produces (along with Kalamata in Peloponnese) most of the Greek olive oil, and to my taste also the best, it is only appropriate that *dolmathakia* is a favourite on the island.

Sitting recently in a little garden on the outskirts of the charming village of Molyvos, on a brilliantly sunlit May morning, just before Greek Easter, with beside me a huge mountain of the freshest of vine leaves resting on the small tin table, I watched the agile ladies of the household (all three generations) dextrously preparing *dolmathakia* while expounding on the merits of their family recipes. Amidst the teasing and reverberating laughter, while the ritualistic, steaming little cups of Greek coffee were circulated, the ritual of the vine leaves itself became a simple but pure source of contentment.

---

225 g (8 oz) fresh or preserved vine leaves, (about 50 if you have a vine in your garden)
150 g (5 oz) long-grain rice, soaked, rinsed and strained

50 g (2 oz) pine kernels (nuts), toasted lightly in a dry frying pan
275 g (10 oz) onions
4–5 spring onions
60 ml (4 tbsp) dill or fennel, finely chopped
30 ml (2 tbsp) fresh mint, finely chopped
45 ml (3 tbsp) parsley, finely chopped
150 ml (¼ pint/⅔ cup) olive oil
juice of 1 lemon
300 ml (½ pint/1⅓ cups) hot water
salt and black pepper

Wash the fresh vine leaves and plunge about 8 at a time briefly, for 1–2 minutes, into a saucepan of boiling water, in order to make them pliable. Take out with a slotted spoon and strain. If using preserved ones, rinse them 2–3 times, and soak them in a bowl of hot water for 3–4 minutes. Take out, rinse again and strain. (Rinse well as they can be extremely salty from the brine they have been preserved in.)

Chop the onions finely or put them through a food processor briefly. Do not purée them. Mix all the ingredients (apart from water), in a large bowl, with half the olive oil and half the lemon juice. Line the bottom of a wide saucepan with vine leaves. Untangle and spread out one vine leaf at a time,

uneven side up. Place a spoonful of stuffing near its serrated end, fold the ends over it, then both sides inwards and roll, forming a cigar-shaped parcel. Place the *dolmathakia* in the saucepan in tight circles, trapping the loose ends underneath. Pour over the rest of the olive oil, the lemon juice, and some seasoning.

Place a small inverted plate over their surface, in order to keep them in place; add the water (they should not be immersed in it), cover and cook gently for 50 minutes.

They can be served hot or cold, arranged on a bed of raw vine leaves, with quartered lemons. Occasionally, plain yoghurt is served with them.

Serves 4.

HTAPOTHI STIFATHO
Casserole of Octopus with Little Onions

One of the best octopus dishes I have ever tried (apart from *htapothi liasto* – sun-dried octopus scorched on charcoal) was a *stifatho* casserole in one of the small *tavernas* at the pretty, colourful harbour in Molyvos, with a group of sunburnt and shrivelled fishermen of that familiar Aegean type, talking about gorgons and singing in the corner. They were ominously dark brown with thin, lined faces, straight noses, black moustaches and stooping bodies, with trousers hanging loosely as if they were a garment alien to the bony structure.

2 small octopus weighing about 1 kg
   (2.2 lb)
150 ml (¼ pint) olive oil
3 cloves garlic, peeled and halved
1 small stick cinnamon
3–4 grains allspice (allspice berries)
30 ml (2 tbsp) red wine vinegar

15 ml (1 tbsp) tomato purée (paste)
   diluted in 300 ml (½ pint/1⅓ cups)
   water
450 g (1 lb) small whole onions, peeled,
   or ordinary onions, peeled and
   quartered
2.5 ml (½ tsp) sugar
black pepper

Wash the octopus properly, particularly around its tentacles, in order to extract the sand. Cover with water, bring to the boil and boil gently for 10–15 minutes, until tender enough to cut. Strain, discarding the water; cut the octopus into bite-sized portions removing its skin as you go. Both tasks should be easy by now.

Sauté the octopus in hot oil until all its water has evaporated and it starts to colour. Add the garlic and spices and sauté briefly, stirring at the same time. Pour the vinegar over and then the diluted tomato purée and some black pepper. Cover and cook for about 15 minutes or until the octopus is almost tender. Spread the onions over its surface, sprinkle on the sugar and rotate the saucepan. Cover and cook gently for 20 more minutes until everything feels very soft but without letting the onions disintegrate. If dealing with tougher octopus, cook them longer before adding the onions and more liquid to prevent them sticking.

Serves 6 as a first course.

SKORTHALIA
Garlic Sauce

This is indispensable in island homes, where it is served with the main course of fried aubergines or courgettes, fried fish or with boiled vegetables such as beetroot. It also makes an excellent *mezethaki* (appetizer). It is best when made with the traditional wooden pestle and mortar (*gouthi*). *Skorthalia* has been consumed in Greece since ancient times and Aristophanes mentions it as a favourite of ancient Athenians under the name *od Skorothalmi*.

3 medium slices crustless white bread, soaked in water for 10 minutes
2–3 cloves garlic, peeled and chopped
15 ml (1 tbsp) white wine vinegar

salt
75 ml (5 tbsp) olive oil
50 g (2 oz) ground walnuts or ground almonds (optional)

Squeeze most of the water from the bread but leave it still quite moist. Place it in a food processor with the garlic, vinegar and salt and blend until smooth. Dribble in the olive oil while the blades are in motion. Add the nuts, if they are to be used, at the end and blend briefly. The mixture should be of a runny consistency. It is served either separately in bowls or spread on top of the vegetables or fish.

Serves 4.

YIEMISTA
Stuffed Vegetables

Since Mytilini is famous for its *ouzo* from the beautiful green village of Plomari, it was inevitable that *ouzathika* would also be part of the tradition. There are a whole range of these little places by the port in Mytilini where one drinks *ouzo* and eats a selection of different but sharply appetizing *mezethakia*, which arrive at the table automatically with each little carafe of *ouzo*, plate after plate. These can constitute a whole meal, which will take hours, as enjoyment, discussion and singing are the prime reasons for going to such a place. Or perhaps a meal will start with a visit to one of these establishments in the capital Mytilini and once the appetites have been titillated enough the group may move to one of the restaurants for a dish of *yiemista* perhaps or an octopus *stifatho*.

For restaurant purposes, large uneven tomatoes and fragrant peppers are mostly used for *yiemista* but in the home, the display will also include small elongated aubergines and maybe courgettes. The *yiemista* can be made with or without the chopped meat.

At the beginning of August when everybody is fasting for the Assumption the following version is the most popular. However, it should be fragrant with the aromas of the hills and gardens.

---

4 large tomatoes and 4 large green
  peppers or substitute 2 small
  aubergines (eggplants) for 2 of these
2.5 ml (½ tsp) sugar
60 ml (4 tbsp) olive oil
15 ml (1 tbsp) tomato purée (paste),
  diluted in 200 ml (7 fl oz/⅞ cup) hot
  water
2 medium-sized potatoes, peeled and
  quartered lengthwise
2.5 ml (½ tsp) dried oregano, preferably
  the wild Greek *rigani*

STUFFING
2 large onions, finely sliced
120 ml (4 fl oz/½ cup) olive oil
1 small aubergine (eggplant), trimmed
  and cubed
225 g (8 oz/1 cup) long-grain rice, rinsed
  and strained
50 g (2 oz) pine kernels (nuts), toasted
  lightly in a dry frying pan
60 ml (4 tbsp) fresh mint, or dill, finely
  chopped
30−45 ml (2−3 tbsp) basil leaves,
  shredded
45 ml (3 tbsp) parsley, finely chopped
salt and black pepper

Oven: 190°C/375°F/Mark 5.

Cut the top off each tomato and pepper and reserve. De-seed (seed) the peppers. Using a teaspoon, scoop out most of the tomato flesh. Chop and reserve it for adding to the stuffing. Invert the tomatoes on a plate to drain them but reserve their juices for adding to the stuffing as well. Sprinkle a little sugar into each tomato before stuffing it. If using aubergines, cut the top off one side and scoop out some of their flesh carefully without piercing their skin. Place them into salted water and leave for 30 minutes. Include their chopped flesh in the stuffing.

To make the stuffing, brown the onions lightly in the hot oil in a frying pan; add the aubergine flesh and sauté for 1–2 minutes. Mix in the tomato flesh and add the mixture to the rice. Add remaining stuffing ingredients and mix well.

Arrange the tomatoes and peppers upright, in a medium baking dish, filling any gaps in between them with the potato slices, which will add a delicious note to the meal. Fill the vegetables without pressing the filling down and seal them with the reserved tops. If aubergines are used, lay them on their sides. Pour over the diluted tomato paste and the oil. Sprinkle with oregano, season and cook for 1 hour and 20 minutes, basting occasionally.

Serves 4.

SARONIKOS

*T*his is the group nearest Athens, the group that we used to visit on school outings for the day or later for weekends. It includes historic Salamis, which not many people regard as an island since it is located so near Piraeus, about 20 minutes away by boat. Its clean pebbly beach of Selinia with simple tavernas offering cheap little crispy fried fish such as *maritha* (baby sardines), *gavros* (fresh anchovies) and boiled wild greens was like Paradise for us in the late fifties and occasionally (I hope neither my teachers nor my parents read this) we would skip school and escape to Paradise on a temporary basis, that is for the day.

The group also contains the island of Aegina, mostly known in the early days for its pistachio nuts and its pretty ceramic hand-painted water carriers (*stamnakia*), which were famous for cooling the water when refrigerators were a rare commodity in Athens. The most beautiful beach on Aegina was that of Aghia Marina – pure sand bordered by a dense pine forest and totally deserted in the late fifties; and nearby on top of a green hill is the 5th-century BC Doric temple of Aphaia Athena. While spending a weekend *al fresco* on this beach in the late fifties, on an uncomfortable bed of pine needles, suddenly, around dawn, it started to thunder wildly and then the heaviest of rains poured down. In the early morning, drenched to the bone, we walked to the nearby village in such a pitiful state that the villagers in a typically hospitable fashion took us in their homes, dried our clothes, made hot *fraskomilo* (wild sage tisane) for us and gave us nice beds for our second night.

Opposite Aegina there is the tiny island of Angistri, which I discovered in the early sixties when very few people knew of its existence. This was almost totally deserted apart from an entrepreneurial lady letting a few rooms in the heart of the forest and cooking for her guests (I still remember her wonderful *keftethes*), and a small local and pitifully poor community at the bare sandy end of the small island. Angistri was the embodiment of an idyll with its pine forests and its little protected emerald bays.

Next there is green Poros with its lagoon-like seas, very near to the Peloponnesian mainland. Then come what we thought of as the 'big islands' when we were small. That is enchanting Hydra and charming Spetsae, both of which forbid cars – a rule that helped to keep the island character pure.

Hydra, rocky and bare of vegetation, has one of the most enchanting and picturesque harbours with the town built like an amphitheatre on the rocks around it. It is a riot of colours with the bright blues and orange colours of the little caiques rocking peacefully, tied in the harbour. Large, beautifully restored traditional houses of the powerful nautical families that originated on this little island are densely built in a honeycomb pattern, rising like a stage set. Walking round her narrow alleys in the spring, with the clean whitewashed courtyards brimming with flowers is a delight, and when the aroma of the honeysuckle is at its most intense, at dusk, it is satisfying to sit in a paved taverna courtyard sipping *retsina* and sampling some of the spring specialities such as *arnaki fricassée* (lamb with cos lettuces).

In the most recent of our visits last year, we walked to the little beach and lovely village at Kaminia, about 30 minutes on foot around the beautiful corniche of the island. We were sustained on the walk by some of the local *amigthalota* (marzipan) that Hydra is famous for. There, at Giorgos' quiet homely taverna, set back a little from the beach, with tables on a cement terrace under a tent, one can have some of the best homely cooking on the island, prepared by Giorgos and his wife, including fish *plaki* and a salad of boiled green *horta*. Neither the walk nor the meal should be missed.

Last comes Spetsae, beautiful and aristocratic, lacking the intense ruggedness but also the unmistakable character of Hydra. Its beautiful neoclassical houses are overhung with colourful climbers. It is here that wealthy Athenians spent their summers while the rather poor intellectual and artistic circles were discovering the simple and frugal Hydra in the early fifties.

COVERED MARKET, CHANIA

SAGANAKI
Fried Cheese

Sit at one of the seafront restaurants in Hydra as dusk descends with an *ouzo* in hand, sampling these golden-fried flat pieces of sharp savoury *kefalotyri* cheese.

◆

45 ml (3 tbsp) corn oil
15 g (½ oz/1 tbsp) butter
150 g (5 oz) *kefalotyri* or Cypriot *haloumi* cheese

lemon quarters to garnish

◆

Heat the oil and butter in a small non-stick frying pan. Slice the cheese into 1 cm (½ in) thick, elongated slices. When the oil is quite hot, but not smoking, arrange the slices side by side in the pan without allowing them to touch as they may stick together. Fry briefly for 1 minute until the cheese starts to get crisp at the sides, then turn each slice over. Fry until light golden, take out and drain on absorbent paper. Arrange on a plate and serve with the lemon quarters.

Serves 4.

ARNAKI FRICASSEE
Lamb and Cos Lettuce (Romaine) Casserole

One of the best Greek dishes, this is found on islands and the mainland alike, around Easter time. It bears a resemblance to *magiritsa*, the soup that breaks the Lent fast after the midnight liturgy on Saturday. It is made with a leg of lamb; however a shoulder can be used, trimmed of excess fat.

◆

1.8 kg (4 lb) shoulder of lamb, boned, trimmed of fat and cubed
1 medium onion, finely sliced
4–5 spring onions, trimmed, washed and chopped
45 ml (3 tbsp) sunflower oil
900 ml (1½ pints/3⅔ cups) hot water
salt

2–3 large cos lettuces (romaine), washed, strained and shredded
60 ml (4 tbsp) chopped fresh dill or 30 ml (2 tbsp) dried dill
AVGOLEMONO-EGG AND LEMON SAUCE
3 eggs
2 large lemons

◆

Rinse and dry the meat. Sauté the onions in the oil until glistening. Turn the heat up, add the meat and sauté, stirring occasionally for about 10 minutes, until all its water evaporates and it starts to stick. Add the water and salt. Cover and cook for 50–60 minutes, until the meat is tender but not falling apart.

Add the lettuce and dill and mix together. Cover and cook gently for 10 minutes. Let the dish stand for 5 minutes before adding the sauce. Using a spoon, skim off as much fat as you can from the surface of the sauce – if it is too greasy it will cause the *avgolemono* to curdle. Beat the eggs lightly. Add the lemon juice and beat together briefly. Gradually add 45–60 ml (3–4 tbsp) of the hot (but not boiling) sauce, beating all the time. Pour the sauce slowly over the meat and stir until well incorporated. Return to a gentle heat for 2 minutes, just to warm the sauce through. Do not allow it to boil, to avoid curdling the eggs.

Serves 4–6.

PSARI SPETSIOTA
Baked Fish in the Style of Spetsae Island

Spetsae, the sleepy little island in the Saronikos Bay near Athens, with its large, traditional neoclassical houses, whose shutters are overhung with brilliant scarlet *bougainvillaea* flowers, has made quite a contribution to Greek culinary tradition with this easy dish of baked fish fragrant with garlic.

Steaks of tuna or swordfish are often cooked in the same manner in Greece and one could improvise and use almost any kind of fish, either in steaks or whole.

---

4 thick steaks of cod or halibut, about 1 kg (2.2 lb), or 4 small whole mackerels
90 ml (6 tbsp) olive oil
2 cloves garlic, finely sliced
60 ml (4 tbsp) parsley, finely chopped

450 g (1 lb) tomatoes, peeled, seeded and finely chopped
salt and black pepper
45 ml (3 tbsp) freshly made toasted breadcrumbs

Oven 190°C/375°F/Mark 5.

Rinse and dry the fish. Arrange it in a medium-sized oiled baking dish. Beat all the ingredients lightly together, apart from the breadcrumbs. Cover each slice or each fish with a layer of the sauce, sprinkle with breadcrumbs and cook for 30–40 minutes, basting occasionally, until light golden and crisp on top.

Serves 4 as a main course with a refreshing, crisp green salad.

DODECANESE

Dodekanisa, as this group is called in Greek, means the twelve islands, but in reality the islands are fourteen and contain large and luscious islands such as Rhodes and Kos, Karpathos and small rocky gems such as Kalymnos, Halki, Kastelorizo, Kassos, Tilos, Patmos, Symi and Leros.

This is the group traditionally associated with fishing and most importantly with sponge fishing. When the local caiques left Kalymnos in the spring on *Kathari Theftera* (Clean Monday) which is the first day of Lent, for their expedition to the African coast, the place reverberated with emotion and farewells. Everybody gathered in the harbour, the local religious hierarchy at the head, reciting the annual blessing, with the women and children watching in silence, almost spellbound by the gravity of the event. The day's traditionally prescribed diet of no animal produce but a frugal meal also matched the sad events.

It is at the smaller islands of the Dodecanese that most traditional colourful customs such as local weddings, the beautiful house interiors of Karpathos and the celebrations of various saints at the particular monastery or church have been preserved to the present day with a unique vivacity and religious fervour. In Karpathos, for instance, the Saint Panteleimon festivity lasts for two to three days while everyone is wined and dined on local specialities such as stuffed lamb and red wine, which local girls offer out of terracotta jugs.

It is in these smaller islands, because of their remoteness, that life is still primitive and innocent. It is here that one can easily slip into the past and lead a life of what might have been.

RHODES

They built for eternity, but they eat as though they were to die to-morrow,
Plutarch quotes an ancient saying about the Rhodians.

('RHODES IN ANCIENT TIMES', Cecil Torr, Cambridge University
Press, 1885.)

According to Greek mythology, when Zeus shared the world among the Gods, he forgot Helios (the Sun). The latter however was content to have for his share a luscious island that he had spotted emerging from the blue sea. The island was Rhodes and sunshine has been its trademark ever since the god happily settled on the island and fathered seven children. The statue of the *Colossus* and the coinage of the island displayed the god's image.

As we drove from the airport to the town, in the warm November sunshine, gardens were dotted with the scarlet and pink of the hibiscus flowers, the roses and the rioting brilliant yellow clusters of the grape-like kassia (acacia) flowers. The air was fragrant with spring aromas and sparkled with the singing of birds. A perfect setting for any arrival. After all, the island derives its name from the ancient Greek word *rothon* (rose) and it instantly justifies it as it gives the impression of a vast garden; an island of flowers.

Among the buildings at the front, facing Mandraki harbour – a setting very *Italianate* – there is a vast arcaded, walled building with its large central courtyard shaded by large trees, which houses the central market. Every morning, in this peaceful garden-like space, the market gets into full swing. Fish of all sizes and hues are displayed in wooden boxes around the central domed kiosk, on stalls and the back of motorcycles. The throaty cries of a seller urge us to buy his tiny lustrous ink-coated *soupies* (cuttlefish). Elsewhere we are urged to buy the furry crabs that are busy trying to escape. The man across the way is busy carving a large tuna while the man next door advertises at the top of his voice the low cost of his wares: pale pink, thin and bony red mullets, extremely cheap because of their diminutive size. Then came the bulgy, big-eyed octopus with

PIGATHIA HARBOUR, KARPATHOS

dark overdeveloped suckers. At that stage, Linda opted for the more genteel and tranquil environment of the vegetable market on the opposite side where she bought two gigantic and absolutely beautiful aromatic quinces. When in need of a break, as we were after a couple of hours, it is extremely pleasant to sit in the sunshine at one of the tables of the *byraries* (small eating places), spread under the trees in the market, have a beer and watch the animated shopping encounters unfold.

But it is the old walled city, the *Kastro*, that will fill you with wonder during the tourist-free autumnal period. Byzantine churches with decaying frescoes of wide-eyed angels, the occasional Turkish minaret added when most of the churches were converted to mosques by the Turkish conquerors, the Gothic buildings with which the Knights of St John stamped the island before they moved on to Malta, all mingle in the cobbled, vaulted, labyrinthine streets resonant with a medieval air. The Order of the Knights of St John, which was established in the 11th century from an assortment of European Catholic nobility, took the island from the Byzantines and ruled it from 1309 to 1522, when the island fell to the Ottoman armies of Suleiman the Magnificent.

The most striking street in Rhodes is the street of the knights which leads to the Palace of the Grand Master with its palm-fringed gardens. An enchanted street in an enchanted city. But my favourite street is Aghiou Fanouriou Street with the eponymous little 13th-century church squeezed between the houses, which breathes melancholy, desolation and decay. (I was always keen on Aghios Fanourios, as on his nameday in the autumn my grandmother, as in most households in Greece, would prepare a huge sweet, spicy cake with olive oil which is called *fanouropitta* – a joyous affair. When it came back from the baker's I would be sent to deliver substantial, diamond-shaped pieces to our neighbours.)

Walking randomly about the old city, one is surprised at each corner by different images; some that are resonant with the past and others with the present. This is not a dead city, but a densely populated one, despite the fact that the main streets have unfortunately been taken over by shops trading in tourist paraphernalia. You will still be pleasantly surprised by the signs of ordinary daily chores: the sweeping of a little garden with potted plants; the aromas of fried garlic emanating from a dark, opened door; a small baker's shop; an elderly lady with inquisitive eyes delivering some freshly cooked delights to a neighbour on a covered plate; a little dark-eyed girl solemnly carrying a hot elongated loaf in her arms like a precious baby; a school in the grounds of a Byzantine church with its elevated yard crowded with noisy little faces; a dark barber's shop and the inevitable *kafenion* (coffee shop) reserved, of course, only for men as custom has it in Greece. If you get lost while looking for one of the innumerable monuments, advice will be dispensed and perhaps a carnation will be pressed through the railings of a courtyard – at once a greeting and a farewell. In Sokratous Street nestles the well-known restaurant of Alexis, a small, charming place with dark wood panelling which only has seafood on offer. It is managed nowadays by the two hospitable and charming Katsibrakis brothers, the sons of Alexis.

Torr says that in ancient Rhodes they judged a man by what he ate. '*A connoisseur in fish was at once pronounced a gentleman: and a man who was content with meat. a mere shopkeeper*'. ('Rhodes in Ancient Times', Cecil Torr, Cambridge University Press, 1885). With that phrase hovering in our minds how could we settle for anything less than a feast of seafood on our first night in Rhodes? Moreover, Athenaeos quotes the poet Lynceus of Samos, who in a letter written around 250 BC praises the island for its fish: its anchovies, grouper and sea urchins, with the prize going to its swordfish. Lynceus also mentions the local custom of eating figs before instead of after dinner, a custom that can still be found nowadays in Italy.

Excitement arrived at our table in the form of a mixed platter displaying the subtle colours of a faded tapestry that consisted of sea-flavoured *kythonia* (clams), for which I have a real passion, lustrous sea urchins (*ahini*), although these were rather small and insignificant and not at their best at this time of the year, and a few greeny-brown knobbly, elongated iodine-flavoured *fouskes* (violettes) with their trembly, yellowish eye-like interior, which I regard as oddities and eat without passion. These were followed by a translucent, exquisitely fresh squid that had been skinned whole and barely cooked over charcoal.

The following evening on Kostas Katsibrakis' suggestion we visited a restaurant in the middle of a pine forest in Tris on the outskirts of Rhodes, called *Kioupia*. It was a miracle that we found it and only then because at the crucial moment, when we realized we were hopelessly lost in the dark forest, we saw the fire of some young scouts camping for the night. Nevertheless a visit to *Kioupia* (a meat restaurant this time) should be one of the priorities while on the island as it is a gastronomic experience; the incredibly wide range of exquisite cold and hot *mezethes* arrives at your table and you only keep the ones you want. The temptation is over whelming so make sure to fast for the day and also to book as it is very popular. In order to enjoy and appreciate all the different

LINDOS, RHODES

charms of the island you will need a car, not only in order to see the exquisite locations of the ancient sights of Ialysos, Kamiros and glittering Lindos but also in order to go off the beaten track to these places and get a glimpse of local life.

The drive to Mount Filerimos to visit Ialysos and feast your eyes on the splendid views from that height, will take you through olive groves and luscious gardens once you have passed the village of Trianda, where men are playing backgammon at a corner coffee-shop or sitting in the sunshine outside the church by the main street. Deliciously crunchy honeyed cakes called *ta hilia tis hanoumissas* (the Turkish lady's lips), bought in a little shop here, were excellent and we went back for more and more.

We left the gem of the island until last: Lindos on the south coast, just waiting for Linda's paint brush. As you take the last crucial turn to your right, high up on the bare hills, suddenly you are dazzled by the unexpected spectacle beneath, your eyes struggling to clear the magic haze in disbelief: Lindos, glittering like a diamond in the sun, white and purely Cycladic. She is crowned by the glimmering beauty of the remaining white Doric columns of the temple of Athena Lindia that have stood on this dramatic location, on her acropolis, unperturbed, proudly facing the sea for over two thousand years. A feast of colours! Lindos has everything; there is nothing she should yearn for, as her beauty has the finality of a perfect but divine circle.

Her beguiling white alleys are studded with houses adorned with highly intricate motifs of Gothic and Islamic detail, the seal of her medieval past; and each high wall reveals a courtyard with an immensely satisfying image of grey and white pebbles. It is in such alleys and such courtyards that one expects to find 'the playful mad pomegranate tree' of the poem by Odysseas Elytis, flirting with the *sirocco* and blooming into a thousand magic dreams.

A ring of magnificent orange groves borders the hillside by the little square where the cars are left. A mass of golden fruit made the branches bend under the weight and in the late afternoon as the shadow of the walled castle fell upon it, it filled the air with the most exotic aromas. In the gardens beneath, throughout the day, people had been gathering their olives, exchanging greetings and teasing their neighbours while eating their frugal lunch under the trees. And on our way back we stopped for an *ouzo* as darkness fell, at the village of Afantou at a local *kafenio* and talked about the specialities of the island to Kyria Maroula Hrisovergi who owns it.

Cumin seems to be the underlying theme both in Rhodes and in Karpathos, while in the other Aegean islands its role is minute; what strange historical connection explains this difference? Is it just the size and the nautical importance of Rhodes that provided her, and consequently her neighbours, with more condiments than other islands?

KYTHONIA STO FOURNO
Baked Quinces

*T*his is one of the most satisfying desserts with its mixture of different tastes, each one creating a different sensation. It is quite common and it is encountered in most fertile islands as well as on the mainland; there is for instance a wonderful version sold by the Athenian supermarkets of Vassilopoulos, freshly baked when quinces are in season.

4 medium-sized quinces, rinsed and dried
60 ml (4 tbsp) granulated or demerara sugar diluted in 50 ml (2 fl oz/¼ cup) water

25 g (1 oz/2 tbsp) butter
15 ml (1 tbsp) granulated or demerara sugar for dusting their tops

Oven: 200°C/400°F/Mark 6.

Place the quinces upright side by side in a small baking dish. Pour the water and sugar into the bottom and dot their tops with the butter. Bake them for about 30–35 minutes until quite tender, basting them 2–3 times. Sprinkle them with the last tablespoon of sugar and cook for another 10 minutes until the sugar has almost caramelized. Serve one per person. As they are quite rich, I would not serve whipped cream with them, but do if you prefer.

Serves 4.

PSAROSOUPA TOU ALEXI
Alexis' Fish Soup

This is the excellent soup served at this charming well-known restaurant in the middle of the old city in Rhodes. It was established in the early fifties by Alexis Katsimbrakis and it is now run by his two sons, who are devotees of good seafood and also extremely hospitable.

It is simple to prepare when your fish is as fresh as theirs. Even though they had intended to use the ferocious-looking bright pink *Skorpines* (Skorpion fish) on the day they planned this meal for us, when their fisherman came back with no such catch in his nets they had to improvise. They chose a shiny and svelte-looking grey mullet, which made an excellent alternative with. an individual taste.

---

1 medium onion, finely chopped
75 ml (5 tbsp) olive oil
600 ml (1 pint/2½ cups) water
1 grey mullet about 1.4 kg (3 lb),
  prepared whole, washed and drained
salt
3–4 small tomatoes, peeled, seeded and
  chopped

2 medium carrots, peeled and quartered
  in 5 cm (2 in) lengths
45 ml (3 tbsp) finely chopped celery
  including some leaves
225 g (8 oz) courgettes (zucchini),
  trimmed, scraped, washed and
  quartered as above
45–60 ml (3–4 tbsp) fresh lemon juice

Soften the onion in the hot oil in a saucepan until it glistens, pour over the water and lemon juice, and when this boils add the vegetables and the fish on top. Cover and cook for about 25–30 minutes, keeping an eye on and testing the fish so that it does not disintegrate. It must hold together so that it can be taken out whole without breaking if possible. Serve the soup with a selection of vegetables on each plate. Serve the fish on a separate platter with remaining vegetables. People can choose either to have the fish with their soup or afterwards. It is a matter of preference really. Offer a bowl of olive oil and lemon quarters for those eating their fish afterwards.

Serves 4.

MOSHARI STIFATHO
Beef Casserole with Baby Onions

We were surprised but absolutely delighted to find this casserole at the little restaurant by the sandy beach on Lindos on a brilliantly warm and sunny day in November. And we honoured it appropriately! It was perfectly cooked by the elderly mother of the owner; the meat was succulent and tender without becoming shred-like, the aroma of spices was fragrant enough to attract all the bees in the area, and the onions were sweet enough to melt in the mouth. All in all it was a great success, even if it sent us to sleep in the sunshine afterwards.

This sharp and appetizing casserole is served either with fried or roast potatoes, but it is also delicious served with creamy mashed potatoes. If you cannot get the small onions you could replace with an equal weight of ordinary onions. Peel them and quarter them and add them to the meat 10 minutes earlier than the little onions and cook gently until perfectly tender and sweet. The onions should on no account be transformed into a pulp.

---

60 ml (4 tbsp) olive oil
60 ml (4 tbsp) corn oil
1 kg (2.2 lb) brisket, skirt or braising
   steak, in large cubes
60 ml (4 tbsp) red wine vinegar
60–75 ml (4–5 tbsp) red wine (optional)
5 cm (2 in) stick cinnamon

5 grains allspice (allspice berries)
small stalk rosemary
900 ml (1½ pints/3⅔ cups) water
salt and black pepper
5 ml (1 tsp) sugar
700 g (1½ lb) small onions, peeled but
   kept whole

Heat the oils in a large saucepan and brown the meat. It will produce a lot of moisture but persevere until it has all evaporated and the meat starts to get golden. Pour the vinegar over it slowly and when the steam subsides add the wine (if you are using). Then add the remaining ingredients apart from the sugar and onions. Mix, cover and cook slowly for about one hour or until the meat is almost tender.

Spread the little onions over the meat and shake the pan to distribute them evenly. If needed at this stage, add a little water, but the casserole should not be swimming in the liquid. Sprinkle the sugar over the onions, cover and cook very gently for half an hour, until the onions are soft but not disintegrating. Do not stir once the onions have been added; rotate the saucepan occasionally to coat them in the sauce.

Serves 4.

KARPATHOS

Quinces hanging on the trees in November, with their pale, unruffled waxy beauty, are like the golden fruit of a surreal, mythological past. Once you have seen them hanging from a bare branch like I did recently in the hills of the enchanting village of Aperi in Karpathos, like an unreal golden trophy amongst the melancholic colours of a landscape, mellow and golden with autumnal sunshine, you will also be left with no doubts as to their golden credentials.

Wrapped in the most exotic aroma they are delicious eaten raw when ripe. Try them peeled and thickly grated, perhaps with a sprinkling of sugar on top and maybe a touch of cinnamon; or they can be made into a compote, sliced, poached and offered with whipped cream at the end of a meal; they are delectable (and for me the best) when baked whole, dusted with sugar and perhaps with a knob of butter; or they can be cooked in a casserole with pork, lamb or beef. And of course they can be made into spoon preserves, jams, or into a gelatinous sheet of paste called *kythonopasto*, that, once dried, is cut into small diamond shapes that can be stored for weeks like confectionery.

Every autumn, it was a very special treat for us children whenever we were allowed to buy a large piece of home-made *kythonopasto*, diamond-shaped and with a sparkling white almond lying across its middle like a dagger lying across its heart, from the wandering seller who would set up shop in the middle of the crossroads of our neighbourhood in the evening, with his huge tray resting on a wooden tripod.

Since we are talking of quinces and quince trees I recall sitting under a beautiful, umbrella-shaped quince tree with its slightly rounded, elegant silvery leaves trembling in the May breeze, heavy with lily-like pink-petalled flowers dropping into our scented cups of tea below. This was in an enchanted garden, in an enchanting village up in north-western Greece in Epiros, in the Zagorohoria.

When choosing quinces, choose ones with a strong aroma and a bright, light yellow colour that shows they are ripe rather than a greenish-yellow hue. Unripe ones, although not bad for cooking with, are inedible raw. If unripe, keep in an airy place for 4–6 days.

It was Elias Zearvouthakis and his wife from Pigathia, the capital of Karpathos, who, among other things, presented us with two beautiful unbelievably-golden quinces which they had just harvested from their garden on the slopes around the graceful old capital of Aperi. The aroma of those quinces was almost haunting.

ARNAKI ME KYTHONIA
Lamb With Quinces

45 ml (3 tbsp) sunflower or corn oil
1.4 kg (3 lb) lean lamb, boned, sliced in large cubes and wiped clean
450 ml (¾ pint/1¾ cups) hot water
salt
2 bay leaves
1.5 cm (3 in) stick cinnamon (optional)

2 large quinces about 1 kg (2 lb), peeled, quartered vertically, cored and kept in a bowl with cold water, to prevent discolouring
45 ml (3 tbsp) granulated or brown sugar dissolved in 300 ml (½ pint/⅔ cup) water

Heat the oil in a large saucepan and brown the meat lightly over a high heat, stirring to prevent sticking. Add water, salt, bay leaves and cinnamon. Cover and cook slowly for 50 minutes, until almost tender.

In the meantime, cut each quince slice into 3 cm (1¼ in) thick elongated pieces. Spread half the slices in one layer in a large frying pan. Pour half of the sugar and water mixture over them and simmer about 10 minutes, turning them over occasionally to coat them in the sugar until all the liquid has been absorbed and they start to turn sugary and brown. Arrange them over the meat and repeat with the remaining quinces in the same fashion. Empty these into the saucepan as well. Turn to cover them in the sauce and, if needed, add a little hot water. Cover and simmer for 20 more minutes, rotating the saucepan occasionally until both meat and quinces are quite tender and most of the water has evaporated.

Serves 4.

MOSHOPOUNGIA
Aromatic Sweet Pastries Filled with Walnuts

One of the numerous happy surprises that awaited us in Karpathos were these pastries offered to us by Elias Zervouthakis and his wife Demetra on 8th November, the celebration of the Archangel Michael. The hospitable Mrs Demetra Zervouthaki was kind enough to let me have her recipe.

These little pastries are filled with delights that could compare to culinary gems. Crunchy walnuts and chopped aromatic candied fruit are enveloped in sweet pastry.

PASTRY

150 g (5 oz/1¼ sticks) unsalted butter
500 g (1 lb/2½ cups) flour, sifted with a pinch of salt and 2.5 ml (½ tsp) baking powder
1 egg
45 ml (3 tbsp) caster (superfine) sugar
30 ml (2 tbsp) *Cointreau* or *Grand Marnier*
60–75 ml (4–5 tbsp) milk

FILLING

225 g (8 oz) walnuts, coarsely chopped

150 g (5 oz) mixed candied (citrus) peel, finely chopped
2.5 ml (½ tsp) grated nutmeg
60 ml (4 tbsp) syrup made from 45 ml (3 tbsp) caster (superfine) sugar and 105 ml (7 tbsp) water

TOPPING

½ teacup (½ cup) rose water
75 g (3 oz/⅔ cup) icing (confectioner's) sugar

Oven: 180°C/350°F/Mark 4.

Rub the butter into the flour, add the remaining pastry ingredients and mix to a rather soft and pliable dough. Cover and leave in a refrigerator for 30 minutes.

In the meantime prepare the syrup. Dissolve the sugar in water over a gentle heat and boil for a few minutes until it has reduced and thickened slightly. Mix the filling ingredients in a bowl and moisten with the syrup.

Divide the pastry into 2–3 sections and roll them out one at a time on a floured surface. Cut out discs of about 10 cm (4 in) in diameter. Place one spoonful of filling across the middle of each one, fold over into a half-moon shape and press the edges together. Place them on a greased baking tray and bake for 30 minutes until pale golden.

As soon as they come out of the oven, brush their surfaces lightly with rose water. Finally dust a platter with icing sugar, arrange them on it in one layer and dust with the remaining sugar.

Makes approximately 15 pastries.

SYMI

'I trata mas i kourelou i hiliobalomeni olo tin eballoname kiolo itan
xeskismeni'
(Our worn-out nets with many patches that we seem continuously to
mend but they always seem to be full of holes.)

(OLD ISLAND SONG).

Like a lace-edged rock, Symi lies in splendour across the water
from Rhodes, unaware of her own startling beauty. Like an innocent maiden carrying on her everyday life, unaware of her magnifi-
cence until by accident one morning she is startled and disarmed
by her own reflection in the garden well.

Small but not unimportant, she made a name for herself along
with Kalymnos as the home of the sponge divers. Her sponge
trade expanded to many European cities, even as far as London
with Symian families starting local business houses. The Symian
sponge divers were constantly improving their technique: in 1840
they were still diving naked with a special stone called a *kam-*
banellopetra tied around their necks. By 1863 they had started to use
diving helmets and weighted suits. The local songs celebrate the
divers' implements in poetry. The diver sings, 'To the sea I owe my
body, to the air my soul but my life hangs on the kambanellopetra.'
But his woman remarks: 'I wish I was a kambanellopetra, hanging
around your neck and filling your heart and thoughts.'

Symi is an island whose people depend upon and occupy themselves with the sea, for the island is almost bare of vegetation apart
from the ubiquitous olive trees and vines. Its menfolk are traditionally fishermen and sponge divers. Island songs, like the above,
about fishermen's and seafarers' lives, their worries, loves and
homecomings abound on Symi.

On Panormitis Bay there is a monastery devoted to the
Archangel Michael the Panormitis, who in the Dodecanese is
considered the patron saint of fishermen and particularly of
sponge divers. His annual festival on 8th November is a glittering

occasion and one of the biggest in the Aegean. It attracts the ecclesiastical hierarchy of the Dodecanese, Despots with their pale, young, bearded novices carrying, for the occasion, the Despots' tall, glittering hats in their black cases. Of course it attracts a flow of people from the archipelago: people from Karpathos, Kassos, Halki, Tilos, Nisyros and Kalymnos make the pilgrimage and every boat in Rhodes, large or small, is filled with several generations of each family, colourful and exuberant, who will make the two-hour journey across for the saint's visit. Mandraki harbour in Rhodes at dawn is a memorable sight, brimming with the same life, zest, and excitement that religious celebrations (*panegiris* as they are called in Greek) used to generate in the old days. Even today a crowd of three thousand people will gather on the hillside of Panormitis' beautiful bay, most of them wined and dined by the monastery, with the local women preparing the feast in the monastery kitchens. The vast dining room and monastical grounds pulsate with life and when there is no more space for even a pin to fall, as the local saying goes, the crowds flow out onto the sunny hillside. We are in the sunniest part of Greece after all.

Throughout the year the fishermen, when invoking the saint and asking his assistance, offer their day's catch to him, in gratitude for their answered prayers. Much of this fish is preserved in salt, in readiness for the feast. On the day of the celebration, after the liturgy, all the celebrants are offered fresh fried fish as well as savoury salted fish rinsed and dressed in local olive oil. Black olives, scarlet radishes and plates of frugal crunchy greenery gathered from the fields, such as sharp, peppery rocket (*roka*), and jugs of light-coloured red wine and cold water will be set out for everyone. Theodore Bent while travelling in the Aegean, around 1883, came upon and commented on at least one such festival on the island of Ios or Nios: '*When hearing of these island festivals, one's thoughts involuntarily travel back to remote antiquity. There are some half-dozen cauldrons piled in one corner of the church, and large wooden spoons with which to stir the contents. Every pilgrim to the festival produces something towards this meal: the well-to-do will bring a lamb or a goat; the*

poor, rice, olives and wine. Everything then is common property and in picturesque groups outside the church they cook their food; into one cauldron is cast the lamb, into another the goat, into another the rice and the fragrance of the meal ascends in wreaths of smoke towards the blue heavens. There is something patriarchal in a scene like this.' This description could perfectly fit the scene of Panormitis.

Not surprisingly, the food of the island revolves primarily around all kinds of seafood, quite often of the most eccentric kind, even on celebratory days such as weddings and baptisms. The fishermen accompany their *mastiha*, a kind of *ouzo*, or their wine with sharp *mezze* such as all kinds of small fish, or whelks without their shells which they preserve in brine, or with hard flakes of salt, including the bag of ink which they extract intact from the octopus and which is called *olos*. Larger fish such as silvery sea bream, Moray eels or octopus are slit open all along their back and sprinkled with black pepper in order to keep the flies away and then dried in the sunshine for a few days. These are called locally *melihlora* and they are extremely popular during Lent. Fish soups abound as do casseroles of fish *plaki*, or *psaria marinata* (fish fried and then immersed in a sharp sauce permeated with the aroma of the rosemary and a little vinegar). You will also find stuffed squid and the most eccentric dish of all, which is the equivalent of a Bolognese sauce made, not with meat, but with finely minced octopus. This adorns pasta on Lenten or other fast days. (Perhaps this dish was a remnant adapted to local customs and needs, left from the Italian occupation of these islands up until the Second World War.) Seafood also figures significantly in local folklore and superstitions. Pregnant women, who occasionally get culinary cravings which can be harmful if unfulfilled, are given a small piece of the dried roe of the octopus which the local fishermen extract and dry in the sun for this purpose. The roe, which is white in colour and looks like a large plate, can sometimes weigh up to 700 g/1½ lb. Once dried, it can be eaten raw like *butargo* or scorched over a flame. The local fishermen believe that it comprises so many flavours that it instantly cures the insatiable craving of the expectant mother.

One of the most significant songs attached to a religious occasion in Greece is sung on 1st January, when children parade from one household to the next singing the *Kalanda*, about the arrival of St Basil – Aghios Vasilis – who usually arrives carrying sweetmeats, writing paper and ink. In Symi he arrives like a fisherman carrying a shallow basket with seafood, whelks and limpets.

Symi town, built like an amphitheatre round a deep turquoise bay, with her ochre neoclassical houses mirrored in the lagoon-like waters, resembles an Aegean Venice with unsophisticated simplicity, or is it a Venice with Aegean sophistication? In either case the town is brilliantly coloured, with each curve and each line clearly defined by the colour of the next.

Steps and more steps, some 375 of them, lead to the upper town, the *Horio*, indispensable to a Greek island. Here you will find decorative wrought iron balconies resting on white-marbled, scalloped cornices; silvery-patterned, pebbled courtyards shaded by overhanging vines and fig trees with dappled light playing on the vermilion of geraniums and the white of oleanders.

Noisy *Kafenia* (coffee shops) by the harbour, are bursting with fishermen and smoke on windy days; mustard-coloured nets drying in the sunshine and further down more being mended, with the little ubiquitous thick white cup of coffee, steaming by the side of the barefoot fishermen. With her startlingly clear emerald-like waters at beaches such as Nos and Pethi, innocent Symi takes her unprepared visitor by surprise with the ease and natural sophistication of her untampered beauty.

KOTOPOULO ME BAMIES
Chicken and Okra Casserole

*T*his is the dish that I always associate with Patmos. Cooked using small okra in one of the restaurants in the alleys behind the harbour it made us go back for more, day after day. Okra adds an exotic unusual flavour to chicken.

1.6 kg (3½ lb) roasting chicken, rinsed
   and cut into pieces
75 ml (5 tbsp) olive oil or corn oil
1 large onion, finely sliced
1 kg (2.2 lb) tomatoes, skinned and
   chopped, or 396 g (14 oz) tin (can) of
   tomatoes

300 ml (½ pint/1⅓ cups) water
15 ml (1 tbsp) oregano (rigani)
700 g (1½ lb) okra
salt and black pepper

Heat the oil in a large saucepan, brown the chicken pieces on both sides over a medium heat and take out. Sauté the onions in the same saucepan until they glisten, add tomatoes, water, herbs and seasoning. Bring to the boil and add the chicken pieces. Coat them well in the sauce, cover and cook for 40 minutes.

Prepare the okra by carefully peeling its conical heads so as not to expose its glutinous juices underneath. Drop them into cold water. Rinse gently and strain. Repeat until the water appears clear. Spread the okra evenly over the chicken. Add a little seasoning, cover and simmer for 30 more minutes or until the okra is tender. Do not stir once the okra has been added, but shake the saucepan occasionally.

Serves 4.

MOUSSAKA
Moussaka

Moussaka has become ubiquitous in the islands. Whether you come across it on Patmos, in Sfakia in Crete or Vathy in Samos, it is one of those dishes which when freshly made can hardly fail. Serve it with a crisp, preferably green, salad as it is quite rich.

MEAT

1 kg (2.2 lb) aubergines (eggplant), trimmed and sliced in ½ cm (¼ in) thick slices

150 ml (¼ pint/⅔ cup) sunflower oil for frying

1 large onion, finely chopped

450 g (1 lb) minced beef or lamb or a mixture of both

396 g (14 oz) tin (can) of tomatoes, finely chopped

1.25 ml (¼ tsp) ground cinnamon or 1 small cinnamon stick

15 ml (1 tsp) dried oregano

salt and black pepper

BÉCHAMEL SAUCE

75 g (3 oz/6 tbsp) butter

75 g (3 oz/¾ cup) plain (all-purpose) flour

600 ml (1 pint/2½ cups) warm milk

salt

40 g (1½ oz/⅓ cup) grated parmesan or Cheddar

1 egg yolk

TOPPING

50 g (2 oz) grated parmesan or Cheddar

30 ml (2 tbsp) freshly made breadcrumbs

Oven: 180°C/350°F/Mark 4.

Immerse the aubergines in lightly salted water for 30 minutes in order to extract their bitterness. Rinse, squeezing them gently, and pat them dry. Reserve two tablespoons of oil; heat the rest and fry the aubergines until light golden on both sides. Drain on absorbent paper to get rid of excess oil.

Meanwhile, soften the onions in the reserved oil in a saucepan; add the meat and sauté until it changes colour, stirring with a wooden spatula. Add the remaining ingredients for the meat. Mix, cover and cook gently for 20 minutes, until the mixture looks drier.

Melt the butter gently in a heavy saucepan, add the flour gradually and stir until well incorporated. Remove from the heat and whisk in the warm milk. Add the salt, return to the heat and keep beating for about 8–10 minutes, until it acquires quite a thick consistency. Remove from the heat, add the cheese and then the egg yolk slowly, stirring continuously all the time. Line a medium-sized baking dish, approximately 26×26 cm (10× 10 in) with the aubergines, seasoning them as you go. Spread the meat evenly on top and cover with the *béchamel*. Sprinkle over the cheese and finally the breadcrumbs. Bake for 50 minutes until golden then let the dish rest for 10 minutes before serving.

Serves 6.

KALAMARAKIA YIEMISTA
Stuffed Squid

Once a local fisherman has consumed three or four little glasses of thick *mastiha* accompanied by all kinds of delicacies extracted from the depths of the sea – perhaps a few spindly sea anemones (*galypes*) looking like an innocent light-brown puffed ball, some sea urchins, or the fresh ink sac of the octopus fried until solidified – he will find his way home through the narrow alleys up into the maze of the little town for a supper that could well feature stuffed squid.

---

1 kg (2 lb) medium squid (3–4)
1 large onion, finely sliced
150 ml (5 fl oz/⅔ cup) olive oil
100 g (4 oz/⅔ cup) long-grain rice, rinsed and strained
60 ml (4 tbsp) fresh dill or parsley, finely chopped

salt and black pepper
juice of half a lemon
30 ml (2 tbsp) tomato purée (paste) diluted in 300 ml (½ pint/1⅓ cups) hot water
15 ml (1 tbsp) finely chopped parsley for sprinkling over

Clean the squid by pulling the heads away from the bodies. Follow instructions on page 36 as for cuttlefish but keep the squid bodies intact. Pull and detach the two little triangular fins on either side of their body. Skin, wash and chop finely for the stuffing. Do the same with the tentacles. Sauté the onion in half the olive oil until light golden, add the finely chopped fins and tentacles and sauté until all the moisture has evaporated and they start to stick. Add the rice, stir to coat in the oil and then add the herbs, seasoning and lemon juice; sauté for 2–3 more minutes and withdraw from heat.

Fill each squid body with this filling, using a small spoon. Do not overfill. Strictly speaking one should then seal the opening at the top using a tapestry needle and thread but this is not vital if one handles them with care. Bring the remaining olive oil and the tomato purée to the boil in a wide saucepan or frying pan that will accommodate the squid in one layer. Add some seasoning and lower the stuffed squid carefully into it. The liquid ideally should not cover them completely. Even if a little filling spills at this stage it is not catastrophic. Cover and simmer gently, occasionally basting the squid with the sauce for about 45 minutes, or until most of the liquid has evaporated and they are coated in a thick sauce.

They can either be served whole or in large segments, garnished with pastry.

Serves 4–6.

CRETE

Crete is vast like the world. Not merely in size, but in the many different elements that combine in her character and fame. Where does an innocent layman start to untangle her myths, her mystery or her beauty? What she is to one person she is not to the next; she is made up of many different dreams.

Walk around the old city in Rethymno, gaze at decaying old wooden doors with the Venetian shields still visible on the yellow porous stone above the entrance and dream about the many faces of conquerors that have passed through the same streets: Saracens, Byzantines, Crusaders, Venetians, Ottomans. Walk around the picturesque Venetian harbour but move on for lunch to the small fishing village of Georgioupolis a few kilometres down the road. Or move east towards Aghios Nikolaos to the village of Platanias and seek out the Voyiatzithakis restaurant, where they make the best of the traditional Cretan wedding pilaf with lamb. Then turn sharply towards the hilly inland among the silvery olive groves bordering the road towards the quaint village of Maroulas. As you travel through the knotted trees, peasant families (if this is the autumn) will probably be hoeing and clearing the ground for the imminent olive picking or laying their plastic netted mats which will catch the tiny local olives as they drop to the earth. The olive trees of the island have had historical and emotional nuances for travellers as well as for their owners.

'I have nowhere remarked earth so deeply red as that of Crete: may it be for this reason that the olive here attains a height and strength far superior to the olive growth in southern France and Italy? Many of the stately trees date from the Venetian times; they may be recognized by their enormous trunks, bent and twisted into a thousand strange and picturesque coils.

('EASTERN LIFE AND SCENERY', Mrs M Walker, London 1886.)

RETHYMNO HARBOUR, CRETE

When you reach Maroulas, you will be surprised by its walled castle-like structures, among the oldest on the island, resembling the homesteads of Mani in the Peloponnese. Walk around its donkey-littered streets and you may even, as we were, be invited into a whitewashed courtyard and offered a little cup of coffee with a cold glass of water from the well.

However, if you are attracted by the sea, you may prefer to make for Georgioupolis. There, with feet splashing in the water, you could sample an exquisite fish soup from the many beautiful specimens that the local fishermen disentangle from their ochre-coloured nets every morning. A dark green, triangular John Dory (*hristopsaro*) with its mysterious round black spots on either cheek or a rosy *skorpina* (scorpion fish), *sfyritha* or brown fleshy *rophos* both of the grouper species.

If you move on to Chania, do not miss a visit to the old decorative iron vegetable market built in 1911. The parade of vegetables and wild greens from the hills, including slender wild asparagus, is exciting and a revelation to the westerner. For colour and freshness, it is a Utopian dream. The most beautiful of all vegetables, the huge local, rose-like globe artichokes with each of their petals ending in a long, elegant thorn, are close relatives of the imperial thistle. Here hang the famous huge, round, yellow Cretan *graviera* cheeses along with the rows of Cretan sausages next door. Then do visit the charming Venetian harbour with its flaky stuccoed façades and sip a little glass of local *raki* and treat yourself to a plateful of ebony-sparkling sea urchins.

If you can visit Crete at Easter, you may experience a Cretan village Easter, which is a traditional event full of pageantry and folklore. Ours was spent with friends at the little hilly village of Episkopi near Rethymno – a village like many other ordinary little villages. We arrived early on the Saturday afternoon and the normally quiet village was in the grip of the Easter fervour with an electric atmosphere. The startling, deafening bangs of fireworks reminded everyone of what was to follow at midnight. People were rushing to and from the only village baker with large round and rectangular aluminium containers filled with the traditional little pastries of the day, the half-moon shaped *skaltsounakia* which are filled with the rich, soft sheep's cheese that each family makes, and the fresh unsalted *myzithra*, polished with egg and decorated with crunchy sesame seeds for the special Easter Saturday dish.

At about 11 o'clock we descended in our finery and stopped for a *raki* (an alcoholic drink made from fermented grape skins after the wine has been extracted), and a plate of tiny, sharp, black, local olives under the huge plane tree at the heart of the village, the local *kafenion* (coffee shop). The earlier deserted village alleys had suddenly come to life as generations of each family could be seen walking abreast, dressed up for the occasion; everyone slowly making their way to the church for the midnight liturgy of the *Anastasi* (the Resurrection). The sad and monotonous ringing of the bell filled the air with gravity and the hope that something on a magnificent scale was just about to take place. The little church square was already crowded with animated groups of people and the new arrivals were treated with excitement as they joined their groups of relatives, friends and peers. The women sparkling in their finery, the children exhibiting their brand new white shoes – indispensable for the occasion. Shortly before midnight, the priests, sparkling and shimmering in their golden finery and jewel-studded basilica-domed crowns, chanting softly and saving their crescendos for the impending dramatic moment, came out into the crisp April night followed by the young boys in the choir, carrying the cherubim, the wide-eyed icons and other sacred and indispensable items to the Greek Orthodox Church.

On the hour of midnight, the monotony of the chanting was shattered into a million tiny fragments by the exuberant burst of the *Hristos Anesti* (Christ has risen), sung in an exhilarated high pitch by the priests and with everyone joining in. At the same time, the crowded space was lit up by a joyful flickering as the previously lifeless large white candles carried by everyone burst into flame and created an air of enchantment with their eloquent dancing shadows. While the priests circle the church three times, singing all the while, the church bells communicate the excitement to the surrounding hillsides, filling the air with wondrous promise. Meanwhile, firecrackers' demonic rage is unleashed, accompanied by the occasional real shot into the air (long forbidden elsewhere by law but a familiar aspect of the ritual in my childhood). Friends and relatives embrace and kiss; the children hide in the folds of their mothers' skirts half-frightened, half-thrilled and definitely overwhelmed; the traditional scarlet hard-boiled eggs emerge from their hiding places in people's pockets as each person takes up his position to crack the eggs. The ritual hierarchy is always taken into account; first will be married couples each with their partner, then children with their parents, those promised or half-promised in matrimony at some future unspecified date. The euphoria is boosted not least by the thought of the celebratory meal waiting at home, after the fasting fervour of the preceding week; a meal whose main focus is the soup called *mayiritsa* that Greeks, including myself, have a passion for and which is made of lamb's intestines, greenery including masses of aromatic dill and finished with an egg and lemon sauce.

The following day, Easter Sunday, which was sparkling with the most beautiful sunshine, we were invited by a local family to the leafy, cool village of Mounthros, about half an hour's drive away, for the Easter lunch – the spit-roasted baby lamb or kid. Mounthros is well known for its natural springs of crystal-like waters which people travel from a distance to sample as they are reputed to have medicinal qualities. Our host's garden was a terrace on the hillside and was shaded by ancient plane trees. The young men of the family were already devoting themselves to the lambs and the older men to making the mezze: the inevitable *kokoretsi*, which consist of the liver, spleen and lungs of the animal cut into mouthful portions and threaded onto long sticks with quantities of garlic and mountain thyme sprinkled over them, then wrapped around with lengths and more lengths of the meticulously cleaned intestines of the animals. These are spit-roasted slowly and the result is so mouth-watering that no feasting gathering in Greece

AGHIOS NIKOLAOS, CRETE

could do without them if it was to be taken seriously by the guests.

With all the generations of the family present, we gathered around a long table while the lambs were deposited in the middle of it to enthusiastic cheers. Once the appetites sharpened by the aromas had been satiated, the matriarch of the household started on a long conversational song with her husband and, occasionally, some of the other guests joined in. These are the traditional *tragouthia tis tavlas*, literally meaning improvized songs, which can be about events in the past as well as in the future.

Going to Crete also means visiting its proud mountains, for which it is famous. There is a wish in Greece for children to grow up and to become as tall as Psiloritis, which is the highest mountain top on the east of the island. Travel through its *Lefka Ori* (White Mountains) and get a glimpse of real Crete, of tall, black-booted, black-scarved shepherds and mountain villages with their apple trees blossoming and their primitive hearths smoking. Descend to the charming bay of Sfakia on the south coast and after sampling some fish in one of the small tavernas by the edge of the sea, travel eastwards at the edge of the *Kethros* mountains through the charming villages of Ano Rothakino kai Kato (the upper and lower Peach) and when you reach the village of Selia stop, like we did, for a hot herb tea at the village square and you will be given an infusion of their *stamnohorto* or *thiktamo* collected on the mountain and fragrantly steaming with cloves.

Immediately below Selia there is one of the most beautiful sandy beaches in Crete, Plakias with the little beach of Damnoni next to it, even more beautiful, bordered with green olive groves and pine trees. Excellent cheese pies made by the local baker on the beach can provide the basis of a picnic with tomatoes and yoghurt; we had ours, after going through the boulders of the breathtaking narrow passage of the Kroutaliotiko gorge just beyond the charming leafy village of Aghios Ioannis with its apple and pear trees dressed up like young brides in starched white flowers. We found the most deserted and dense olive grove carpeted with yellow daisies, and by the waters of a stream at its edge we devoured the tight, sharp olives that our hosts had provided us with and some lovely salty white cheese along with the rest of the items of our improvised picnic, which tasted absolutely sumptuous under the hot April sun.

On a route like this the many faces of Crete unfold with an astonishing precision. Travelling on, towards the *Kethros* mountains you will go through such beautiful mountain villages as *Aghios Vasilis,* where we stopped and talked to some black-clad ladies gathering the heart-shaped leaves of the fragile climber called *avronies,* which they were going to cook with snails. They chatted excitedly and explained that *avronies* are also eaten on their own; they are sautéed with olive oil and then a thickening batter of vinegar and flour is added before they are consumed. But the list of wild *horta* gathered from the hills is endless and exotically named: *gourounopothis* (the pig-footed), *stamnagathi* (the pot-thistle), *koutsounathes* (the little dearest), *tzilibithia* (flibbertigibbets or something of the sort), *hatzikous* (Mecca pilgrims), *stafylinaki* (a sage plant whose little round green bobbles are eaten like fruit), the juicy and refreshing, wild asparagus, and herbs such as mint locally called *valsamo* (balsam), wild dill, etc.

The ladies were so hospitable that they invited us for the snail and *avronies* lunch, which unfortunately we could not attend. The previous day we had been offered bunches of wild asparagus from another lady and further down we were offered the whole crop that two other ladies had been collecting all morning among the tangled undergrowth of the deserted fields. This is Crete: wild but magnanimous, proud but hospitable, beautiful but also charming, and, above all, human.

Although her beauty may be found on such famous beaches as palm-fringed Vai or sparkling white, caved Matala, or amidst the ruins of her ancient palaces in Knossos among the figurines of straight-nosed princes bearing lilies, it is far away from these that the real Crete will be found.

SKALTSOUNAKIA
Little Cheese Pies

There are different versions of these little pies; some are made with wild greens, *horta*, gathered from the hills, sautéed and mixed with cheese; others are made with cheese alone. The following version was made with the sharp, tasty, home made sheep's cheese, the *xynomyzithra* as it is called. You can substitute some tasty *feta* for this. They make an excellent *mezethaki* (appetizer), or they will add variety to a frugal table of a vegetable casserole or a thick soup.

PASTRY
350 g (12 oz/2⅔ cups) plain (all-purpose)
    flour, sifted with a pinch of salt
30 ml (2 tbsp) olive oil
60–75 ml (4–5 tbsp) cold water
FILLING
5–6 spring onions, trimmed and
    chopped or 1 medium onion, finely
    chopped

45 ml (3 tbsp) olive oil
275 g (10 oz) *feta* cheese, crumbled
1 large egg, lightly beaten
60 ml (4 tbsp) chopped fresh mint or
    15 ml (1 tbsp) dried mint
black pepper
sunflower oil or corn oil for deep frying

Make the pastry by mixing the ingredients together and kneading vigorously. Cover and let it rest at room temperature for half an hour. Roll it out thinly, onto a floured surface, and cut out small circles approximately 10 cm (4 in) in diameter, using a pastry cutter or a saucer.

Sauté the onions in the hot oil until glistening. Mix them with remaining ingredients in a bowl. Place a heaped spoonful of filling in the middle of each pastry disc, fold over and press the two edges firmly together, forming a half moon shape. They can wait at this stage for about an hour.

Place enough oil in a large frying pan to reach about 3 cm (1¼ in) up the sides; heat the oil properly and fry them over medium heat for 1–2 minutes on either side, turning them over once, until pale golden. They are best eaten immediately, but they are also good cold the following day if there are any left over.

Makes 12–14 pies.

RYZOGALO
Rice Pudding

Courses of cold fish (cuttle-fish and red-mullet) followed next and then came the rice and milk pudding (risoglio) with an elaborately stencilled pattern of grated nutmeg on top.

('THE CYCLADES', J. Theodore Bent, London 1885.)

The *ryzogalo* of the passage was offered to Bent and his wife on the island of Foleganthros, but it has always been popular in the islands. Sit at the waterfront (not only in Foleganthros) in the Venetian harbour in Rethymno in the early afternoon and have a bowl of *ryzogalo*, while your eyes are feasting on the colours and shapes of the small boats jostling in the harbour with the sand-like castle rising at the far end.

---

75 g (3 oz/½ cup) short-grain rice, washed and strained
210 ml (7 fl oz/⅞ cup) hot water
450 ml (¾ pint/2 cups) milk
70g (2½ oz/⅓ cup) caster (superfine) sugar
7.5 ml (1½ level tsp) cornflour (cornstarch) diluted in 90 ml (6 tbsp) cold milk

4–5 drops pure vanilla essence or 10 ml (2 tsp) rose water
1 egg yolk, lightly beaten
2.5 ml (½ tsp) cinnamon for sprinkling on top

Cook the rice in the water until most of it has been absorbed. Add the milk, and cook gently, half-covered (to stop it boiling over), for 20 minutes. Add sugar, cornflour, vanilla or rose water and cook for 5 more minutes. Remove from the heat and let it cool slightly. Add the egg slowly, stirring until well amalgamated; return to very gentle heat just for a few seconds. Serve in small bowls immediately before it sets and sprinkle cinnamon on top. It can be eaten hot or cold.

Serves 4.

VIEW OF CHANIA HARBOUR, CRETE

ANGINARES ME KOUKIA
Globe Artichokes with Broad Beans

*I*n Crete they serve this with wonderful thick-crusted sheep's yoghurt. Seek out the frugal little restaurants around the market in Aghios Nikolaos and you may be rewarded with this dish.

---

juice of half a lemon
4 firm globe artichokes
5–6 spring onions, trimmed, washed and chopped
120 ml (4 fl oz/½ cup) olive oil
700 g (1½ lb) fresh young broad beans

3–4 whole small potatoes, peeled
juice of 1 lemon
salt and black pepper
5–6 *maratho* (fennel) tops or 60 ml (4 tbsp) chopped fresh dill

---

Have ready a bowl of cold water with the juice of half a lemon squeezed into it. Drop the artichokes into it as you finish preparing each one in order to prevent them from discolouring.

Pull and discard about three-quarters of the hard outer leaves of the artichokes from their base until the tender inner ones appear. Always use a stainless steel knife to prevent discolouring, cut horizontally at the middle of the collar of leaves and discard the upper part. Cut and keep the extra length of stalk, leaving about 8 cm (3 in) attached to the artichoke; trim stalks of their hard green outer coating. Slice the artichoke horizontally into two, exposing its inner heart. Using a small stainless steel spoon scoop out the hairy choke and discard, including the brittle, small, purple leaves round it. Next pare off the base of the hard green coating and drop them into the bowl.

Shell the beans; keep the smaller ones whole, removing their sides with a sharp knife. Rinse and strain.

Sauté the spring onions in the hot oil using a large saucepan. Add beans and potatoes and stir to coat in the oil. Pour the lemon juice over, add the artichokes and enough hot water to reach their top. Add seasoning and dill, cover and cook gently for 50 minutes, stirring and turning occasionally until quite tender.

Serves 4.

FASOLATHA
Cannellini Bean Soup

*F*asolatha, of course, is *the* national Greek dish, much loved on the mainland but particularly so on the islands, where it is as ubiquitous as the olive. One will find variations from island to island, for instance on Santorini they add coarsely chopped *seskoula* (a kind of Swiss chard) and in Corfu, where the Italian influence is most prominent in all aspects of life, they add what else but pasta!

The soup is not only delicious and extremely nourishing but also one of the easiest dishes to prepare. Good olive oil is vital to the flavour of the dish, so there should be no economizing on that front.

---

225 g/8 oz cannellini beans or haricot (white) beans, picked over and soaked overnight
1 medium onion, finely sliced
2 carrots, thinly sliced
1 stalk celery, trimmed, washed and finely sliced
396 g/14 oz tin (can) of tomatoes, chopped

15 ml (1 tbsp) tomato purée (paste)
5 ml (1 tsp) each of oregano and thyme
150 ml (¼ pint/⅔ cup) olive oil
900 ml (1½ pints/3⅔ cups) water
salt and black pepper
45 ml (3 tbsp) chopped parsley

Rinse and strain the beans. Put them in a large saucepan, cover with water, bring to the boil and cook for 3–4 minutes. Strain, discarding the water. (This step safeguards against flatulence and makes the beans digestible.)

Put beans back with 900 ml (1½ pints) fresh water. Bring to the boil and add the remaining ingredients, except the parsley.

Cover and cook for about one hour, or until the beans are soft but not disintegrating. If using a pressure cooker, which is ideal for the dish, cook for 4–5 minutes only under 6.8 kg (15 lb) pressure. Finally add the parsley and heat through.

Serve with olives and taramosalata.

Serves 6.

ORANGE GROVES, CRETE

THE IONIAN
ISLANDS

*Setting out on the journey to Ithaca, you must pray that the way be long,
full of adventures and experiences. The Laistrygonians and the Cyclops,
angry Poseidon do not be afraid of;*

('ITHAKA' FROM 'POEMS' by C. Kavafis, Ikaros, Athens 1965.)

Our journey is nearing its completion but not its end as this may
spark more journeys, either to Kavafis' Utopian Ithaka or to the
very island of Odysseus and Homer. It makes no difference as long
as one arrives at the destination full of the knowledge and the
exultation of the experiences on the way.

These are the islands that have gained fame for their lusciousness and esteem for their unique culture. Their musical tradition –
tuneful, cultured and mannered – is instantly identifiable with a
melodic softness found nowhere else in Greece. The group
includes first and foremost glittering Corfu, beguiling Paxi with the
little island of Antipaxi like glittering twins, beautiful Kefalonia,
charming Lefkas, mysterious Ithaca and capricious Zante. The first
image they evoke is of a landscape groomed rather than bare and
exposed to the dazzling sun such as the one of the Aegean islands.
They are blessed with much more rain, if this is regarded as a
blessing, as the locals in Corfu constantly complain about their
rheumatism. As a result the Ionian is a sea virtually choked in olive
groves with no scarcity of olive oil and each household, with no
exception, will harvest their own. Their culinary themes are also
different as they follow the historical patterns of this area which
had been mainly under Venetian rule, but had also experienced the
French and British rule.

CORFU

*Though the olive is an undependable friend its role never varies; dipped
into it, the coarse peasant bread tastes dense and foul – yet the children of
the fishermen have warm brown skins and dazzling white teeth.
Everything is cooked in it.*

('PROSPERO'S CELL', Lawrence Durrell, Faber and Faber,
London 1975.)

As the small planes come down to land over the lagoon-like waters
of the peninsula of Kanoni the landscape unfolds rapidly in an
impressive sequence. Nature reclines underneath in a luxuriant
existence with her voluptuous curves in full view, a case of natural
and unintended exhibitionism. A *collage* of warm blues and
metallic iridescent greens. These were my first impressions of
Corfu in the early sixties on almost daily flights to the island.
Within seconds, enchantment glides underneath as the toy island
of Pontikonisi (Mouse Island) with the 12th-century church of
Pantokrator (the Almighty) flashes its beauty to the sky.

The *Phaeakes*, the ancient inhabitants of the island, were, according to Homer, a happy, gentle and cheerful lot whose love of
music, dancing and enjoyment made them the favourite of the
Olympian gods. The same could not be a more accurate description of the modern inhabitants. The local people seem to have been
groomed by the gaiety and gentleness of their landscape. The term
Kerkyraios (an inhabitant of Kerkyra or Corfu) during my childhood
had undertones of gaiety, song and dance.

Linda and I were in Kerkyra town on the first Sunday of November, the Protokyriako as it is known locally. This is a unique
Sunday, one of four throughout the year when the relic of the
patron saint of the island, Aghios Spyrithon (St Spyrithon), is
paraded along the elegant, leafy front near the *Spianatha*
(Esplanade). The custom originated during the Venetian occupation of the island to commemorate the island's deliverance from
famine, the plague, and finally the Turkish armies, through the
Saint's miraculous intervention. The oldest of these celebrations is

the one on Holy Saturday, on which day the island was saved from famine at an unknown date. Boats loaded with grain bound for Venice met with such a storm that they sought refuge on the island, where they were stranded for a month and had to sell their provisions to pay for their keep. The celebrations on Palm Sunday and the first Sunday in November both commemorate deliverance from plague epidemics in 1629 and 1673 and the one of 11th August commemorates the repulse of the Turkish fleet in 1716.

On the Sunday morning before the procession was due at 11, we sat in a prominent position in the corner of the Café Capri on the wonderfully elegant arcaded front called *liston* because of the lists of noblemen that were meticulously held in the same building during the Venetian occupation. *Liston* has a pleasant gracious air and with the dense acacia trees just opposite it makes a unique spot to sit and have a coffee on a sunlit Sunday morning when families parade after church in their smartest outfits. As this was not an ordinary Sunday, people soon started to gather from villages all over Corfu, some old ladies still displaying their colourful traditional outfits with long, dark skirts, white blouses and their ornate, starched, dazzling white headdresses. Soon the captivating performance unfolds in the brilliant sunshine. First come the bands: one dressed in bright scarlet with shining silver helmets, another in dark blue with burgundy stripes on the sides of their trousers and shining golden helmets, another one with dark blue and purple decorations, one in muted grey; then the golden faded relics with the young boys of the choir, and the bishops in their sparkling satin and gold outfits with jewel-studded golden crowns; the school children and finally the golden-domed cask with the Saint's remains.

However, Kerkyra is not only a uniquely musical city but also an elegant one with faded ochre *stucco* buildings dominated by elongated overlapping dark green shutters, a proof of her Venetian past. From the Byzantines, then the Normans, Kerkyra was eventually taken by Venice, who had coveted the island for some time. The Venetians ruled from 1386–1797, for over 400 years. The Italian

THE MARKET, CORFU TOWN

influence from this period is still noticeable today in more than one aspect of her life and not least in the local cooking. But since the island was briefly occupied by the French and the British, glimpses of their culinary traditions can also be traced. The cookery repertoire is compiled from a mixture of Italian sources which have been overtly Hellenized. The tomato, the favoured ingredient of Mediterranean cooking and southern Italy, is almost as absent here as it is in the Venetian kitchen, although garlic has infiltrated the genteel ranks as Greeks, since antiquity, have been too attached to it to desert it. Here you can find *pancetta* (unsmoked bacon or in this case pig's lard) which is added to beans and other dishes, *makaronchini*, *cannelloni* and pasta of all kinds, *bourdounia* a sausage identical to the French *boudin* from which it derives its name, fish *savoro* that is preserved in a sweet and sour sauce with currants and rosemary, this being the speciality of this particular November Sunday, even the famous Venetian *risi e bisi* (a soup of rice and the first sweet peas) which was the dish that opened the dinner given by the Doges in honour of St Mark on 25th April in the Republic of Venice; although locally it is different from the authentic Venetian soupy dish, as it is a dish of meat served with rice, peas and carrots.

The local specialities which are unique to this part of Greece also bear Italian-based names: *Bourthetto*, *Sofrito*, *Pastitsatha* are self-evident. And an extraordinary dish that made me laugh a lot on the evening we were invited for dinner by the hospitable family of Kostas Zohios is *avga a la bagno Maria*. This, Kostas and his wife claimed, was an excellent and light dish for an evening meal which was a real favourite in the old days. After a little prodding, it turned out to be eggs poached in water, olive oil and lemon and served in their liquid like a soup; it had obviously derived its name from the French cooking utensil *bain marie*. As for the local soups, in pure Italian fashion they featured on every restaurant menu daily and resembled the Italian *minestrone* rather than the Greek *avgolemono*. As a local said, when he has soup in Athens, he has to dive into it in order to find anything more substantial than water.

And in the busy *candounia* of Kerkyra's commercial centre

around Aghiou Vassiliou Street there is a small but charming central market which operates daily. Here you'll find fresh fish displayed on sloping wooden counters or elongated wooden boxes; an abundance of small silvery sea bream (*kefaloi*), then *koutsomoures* (an inferior version of red mullet, much paler in colour); a shop specializing only in tuna, unusual creamy looking prawns that are served fried, tiny inky cuttlefish, octopus and more octopus of all sizes; fresh opaque-grey squid, a huge and threatening sword fish and large creamy-pink cockles with elegant short spikes on their shells, known locally as *alithines* (the real ones). The vegetable stalls are also a delight with the eccentric white beetroot. This is a bunch of greens with a thin white root which tastes faintly of beetroot, rather than the scarlet bulbous roots we are used to elsewhere. You can find an infinite variety of *horta* (wild and cultivated greens), with an exquisite freshness: *frykalithes*, *rathikia*, tasty spinach, *curly endives* and baby courgettes crowned by magenta-tinted creamy flowers. The most beautifully perfumed bunches of *muscatel* grapes set off the perfectly golden quinces still covered with the softest layer of transparent fur like a newborn baby's head.

Across the road there is the only remaining shop of a unique kind, clearly a relic of the days of British rule. It is basically a 'fish and chips' shop but without the 'chips'. Tasos Priftis, its owner, has been frying fish in huge cauldrons for 27 years and his father had done the frying for the previous 20 years. He fries red mullet, cuttle-fish, prawns, squid or whatever the market offers on the day. These are sold by weight. Not long ago the market had five more shops of the same kind that did not only fry fish but also items that are indispensable to a Greek table, such as aubergines.

What mainly distinguishes the luscious landscape of the island is the abundant presence of the old but beautifully twisted olive trees and the dark green, slender cypresses that defiantly stretch their elegant figures from the rioting undergrowth of the soft-curved hills towards the fragile blue of the sky. Walk down to the enchanted *Myrtiotissa* beach, or treat yourself to the unique iridescent sunset from the village of *Pelekas*; or walk at a leisurely pace from the main road to the Achillion Palace in the luscious heat of the deserted November afternoon, through the wild autumnal flowers; the strangely shaped bushes of the prickly pears, the luscious soft green of the huge walnut trees, the olive trees, the trailing geraniums in all shades of pinks, the scented flowering jasmin tumbling over stone village walls, and the bright-eyed pelargoniums. When the heat becomes intense, stop at a little local *kafenio*, which the men have deserted at this time of the day, in the little sleepy village of Gastouni whose village houses are covered with the rioting flowers of the bougainvillaeas and have a cold drink or a Greek coffee and a chat with the elderly owner. Once you reach the top, stand in the high gardens of the Achillion Palace among the purple bougainvillaeas, the scarlet hibiscus, the white daisies and the golden marigolds (not a bad display for early November) and take a sweeping look inland or down the rolling hillside towards the glittering blue Ionian sea to fill yourself with peace and contentment and feast your eyes on tranquil splendour. Paradise must have been designed similarly.

KOFINETTA, CORFU TOWN

PASTITSATHA
Spicy Braised Beef

This is the celebratory meal of the Corfiotes, reserved for special occasions and large family gatherings. This is the recipe of Kyria

Spyrithoula Zohiou, who is praised among her relatives for the excellence of her *Pastitsatha*.

---

3 cloves garlic, peeled and finely sliced
2.5 ml (½ tsp) ground cinnamon
1.25 ml (¼ tsp) ground cloves
salt and black pepper
1.4 kg (3 lb) top rump roast or rolled brisket
45 ml (3 tbsp) olive oil

15 g (½ oz/1 tbsp) butter
4 large onions, peeled and sliced finely
30 ml (2 tbsp) tomato purée (paste), diluted in a little hot water
30 ml (2 tbsp) red wine vinegar
500 g (1 lb) spaghetti

Oven: 170°C/350°F/Mark 3.

Mix the garlic with the cinnamon, cloves, salt and pepper in a little bowl. Make frequent deep slits around the meat and fill them with some of the garlic mixture, pressing it down inside the meat until it is all used up.

Heat the oil and butter, preferably in a large ovenproof casserole. Sauté the meat until lightly brown all over and remove. Add the onions and stir until lightly brown. Put the meat back into the saucepan, add enough hot water to barely cover it, the tomato, salt and pepper, cover and cook slowly, turning the meat over frequently and stirring the onions to prevent them sticking, until the meat is tender. This will take about 1½ hours. Alternatively cook in a pre-heated oven for 2 hours, turning the meat and stirring the

onions as before. When the meat is tender and most of the moisture has evaporated, put the pan on the heat.

Pour the vinegar slowly over the meat and let it bubble for 5 minutes uncovered, making sure that the onions don't stick. By then, you will have a deliciously reduced sauce, smooth and sweet with the melted onions. If the sauce has not reduced enough, take meat out and cook the sauce rapidly, uncovered, until it is reduced. Discard the string, slice the meat and put it back into the sauce.

Cook the *spaghetti* in plenty of water until *al dente*. Serve immediately with the sauce over the pasta and the meat on the side.

Serves 6.

FRYGATHELIA
Little Liver and Garlic Parcels

*L*efkas, still quite traditional with its village ladies dressed in their dark local costumes, offers lovely fresh fish from her emerald sea, and simplicity and friendliness from her people. Apart from these though, she offers *frygathelia*, one of the most enticing *mezethes*. The name is derived from the Italian word for liver, *fegato*. These small parcels of liver are wrapped in caul (the Greek *bolia*), which is the lining of the stomach. They are served either fried, grilled on charcoal or roasted in the oven. They are easy to prepare and the result is sumptuous. Eat them at once.

Also particularly delicious are the local sausages, which are hung to dry in the air. Pies of all kinds are made and the traditional bean soup (*fasolatha*) is made in Lefkas with no tomatoes, as is the lentil soup. *Skorthalia* (garlic sauce), always a favourite of Greek islanders, is made in the Aegean with soaked stale bread, while in the Ionian it is made with boiled potatoes, which are mashed with some water before the remaining familiar ingredients are incorporated. This is served with fried fish, particularly tuna, as we sampled it at the lovely fishing village of Nythri after visiting the monastery of *Faneromeni* up in the hillside, outside Lefkas. From *Nythri* one can see the small private island *Mathouri*, where the poet Valaoritis lived, and also the little island of Skorpios, which belongs to the Onassis family.

---

275 g (10 oz) calf's liver, thickly sliced
2 cloves garlic, crushed
salt and black pepper
30 ml (2 tbsp) finely chopped parsley

2–3 large pieces lamb's caul, rinsed
sunflower oil for frying
lemon quarters to garnish

Slice the liver into pieces about 10 cm (4 in) long and 5 cm (2 in) wide. Mix the garlic, a little salt, a lot of pepper and the parsley and place a thin line of this mixture along the length of the centre of each slice. Place the caul in a bowl of warm water to make it pliable; cut pieces off the caul slightly larger than the liver and stretch each one gently as it tears. Roll up each slice of liver and wrap it as neatly as possible in a piece of caul, forming a short, stout cigar. Secure with a toothpick and refrigerate until ready to eat.

Heat a little oil in a frying pan and fry the parcels gently but briefly, for about 2–3 minutes altogether until light golden all over. Discard the toothpicks. Slice each parcel thinly, sprinkle lemon juice over them and serve.

Serves 4.

VYSINATHA
Sour Cherry Preserve

While we sit here Ourania the heavily made but beautiful peasant girl
comes out in her bare feet, the corner of her blue headdress gripped
modestly between her white teeth, and arranges glasses of Visino before
us; 'Would'st give me water with berries in't?' says the Count reflectively
– 'have I never told you that Corcyra is Prospero's island? This,' he
indicates the glass in which Ourania has placed a spoonful of dark viscous
raisin jam, 'is one of the links in my chain of reasoning. I cannot think
that the scholars would support me, but you my friend,' turning to
Zarian, 'you would take a little pleasure in the knowledge that
Shakespeare was thinking of Corcyra when he wrote The Tempest. *Who*
knows? Perhaps he even visited it.'

('PROSPERO'S CELL', Lawrence Durrell, Faber and Faber,
London 1976.)

Vysinatha, glittering with its dark ruby colour in a tall glass, opaque with icy water, is offered to the visitor throughout the summer, not only in the Ionian Islands but also in the Aegean. It is cooling, soothing and mesmerizing with its sugariness. The visitor, glass raised in one hand, toasts his hosts, drinking a little of the cooling contents, then eating a few of the *berries (vysino)* with his spoon and drinks again to wash their numbing effect from his palate.

Vysino is the most common of the spoon preserves and no household in Greece can survive without it. Offered on its own, over vanilla ice cream or over yoghurt, it always constitutes a treat.

Normally the formula is of equal amounts of fruit and sugar, but if the household is aiming to have extra fruit juice for this refreshing drink then extra sugar is added as in the recipe below. The sour cherry season is quite short and keeps the women busy for 1–2 weeks around the middle of July.

---

1 kg (2 lb) sour cherries
180 ml (6 fl oz/¾ cup) water

1.5 kg (3 lb/6¾ cups) caster (superfine) sugar

Wash and stone the cherries over a bowl in order to catch their juices; place their pits in a little bowl with the specified amount of water so that no juices are wasted. Strain and discard the pits and place the strained water, with the cherries and remaining ingredients, in a large saucepan. Stir over a gentle heat, bring to the boil and skim the froth that rises to the surface, until clear.

Cook uncovered for about 20 minutes until the cherries are soft. Now test for setting; drop a little of the preserve onto a cold saucer and if it is not too runny and forms a light film on top, setting point has been reached. Withdraw from the heat and let it cool. Lift the cherries out with a slotted spoon and store in clean, dry glass jars. Store the juice in clean, dry bottles. Seal and keep in a cool place.

The preserve keeps indefinitely and even if it goes hard and sugary at a later date, the situation can easily be remedied. Empty it into a saucepan, add 60 ml (4 tbsp) boiling water and the juice of half a lemon, stir and bring to boil gently. Let it bubble for 1–2 minutes until completely diluted. When cool, store as before.

Serve 45–60 ml (3–4 tbsp) of juice, diluted in a glass of cold water. Alternatively you can add a spoonful of the cherries in the glass as well, or serve the cherries separately.

A COTTAGE, LEFKAS

KREATOPITTA KEFALONITIKI
Kefalonian Meat Pie

Beautiful Kefalonia, as the popular song goes, lies in the arms of her deep blue sea. Kefalonia displays the typical natural charms of the Ionian and has some lovely villages and beaches. The most beautiful villages are the picturesque Fiskartho with its whitewashed houses set against the cypress-studded hills in the background and the village of Assos in its unique location, tumbling down the hillside with its faded terracotta rooftops to its lagoon-like emerald waters. I have a friend in Athens who was so taken by these two villages that now a summer cannot pass without her visiting them.

The traditional cookery of the island is a history of pies of all kinds. In the past, these pies were mostly made with salted and preserved fish such as the pie with the eccentric name of *kofisi*. *Kofisi* is dried fish which is first pounded, then soaked in changes of water for 2–3 days to reconstitute and soften it and finally boiled. Once it has cooled down, it is shredded and mixed with onion, garlic, short-grain rice, 1–2 tomatoes, olive oil and its own stock to make the pie filling. Pies are occasionally made with salted cod.

However, Kefalonia is famous for another pie, a delicious meat pie, which is the traditional meal during the exuberant celebrations of Greek carnival in February or March but also at large family gatherings and religious celebrations. This is made mostly with goat's meat, preferably from a nanny goat; or with beef, occasionally mixed with a little lean pork. The meat is mostly cooked the previous day as it requires long simmering, but most importantly it makes it a less laborious task. Although the local women in Kefalonia make their own shortcrust pastry, you can successfully substitute ready-made paper-thin *fyllo* pastry. This recipe comes from Kyria Stavroula Glykopanti, from Kefalonia, the mother of one of my best friends.

1 kg (2 lb) of boned lean brisket of beef, or lean lamb, cubed
2 medium onions, finely sliced
2 cloves garlic, peeled and crushed
90 ml (6 tbsp) olive oil
2 eggs, lightly beaten
50 g (2 oz) short-grain rice, rinsed and drained

100 g (4 oz) white *feta*, crumbled or *gruyère* cubed
1 large tomato, peeled and finely chopped (optional)
2.5 ml (½ tsp) ground cinnamon
salt and black pepper
PASTRY
500 g (1 lb) *fyllo* pastry
150 g (5 oz/1¼ sticks) butter, melted

Oven 180°C/350°F/Mark 4.

Cover the meat with cold water, bring gently to the boil and skim until clear. Add the seasoning, cover and cook for 1 hour 15 minutes or longer until perfectly tender. Strain the meat, reserving the juices.

Sauté the onion and garlic in the hot oil until just pale golden and empty into a large bowl. Add the remaining ingredients including the meat and enough juice to make it quite moist.

Choose a large roasting dish approximately 28×39 cm (15×11 in) and butter it liberally. Butter each layer of pastry and spread it according to instructions on page 53. When half the pastry has been used, spread the filling evenly over it and cover neatly with remaining pastry. Butter the top and using a sharp knife cut parallel lines about 8 cm (3 in) apart to mark the top layers of pastry only. Cook for 50 minutes. Take out and let the pie rest for 10 minutes before cutting in elongated or square pieces. Serve with a crisp green salad.

Serves 6–8.

BOURTHETO
Fish Casserole with Cayenne *Pepper*

A favourite way of cooking fish at home in Corfu. Smaller fish are ideal. Allow one per person and always keep them whole with their heads intact as they add flavour to the sauce. (Greeks regard fish heads as the most succulent part and they leave them till the end, as a treat. A fish head is not discarded until it has been properly sucked.)

Other whole fish can be cooked in the same way. Try small mackerel, hake or gurnards. We tried an excellent *bourtheto* in the hospitable home of Spyrithoula and Kostas Zohios. On that day, the central market in the crowded old commercial part of the city displayed an abundance of fresh, silver shiny small grey mullets, so this is inevitably what Kyria Spyrithoula had used for our meal. She also uses red skorpion fish when available. *Bourtheto*, our hosts pointed out, is a dish that requires wine, preferably light red and local like the wine we had at their house which came from a friend's vineyard. Fresh bread is needed for the sauce.

1 kg (2 lb) small grey mullet *kefalous* prepared whole or 1 large one cut in steaks
salt and black pepper
90 ml (6 tbsp) olive oil
2 medium onions, finely sliced

15 ml (1 tbsp) tomato purée (paste), diluted in a little hot water
2.5–3.75 ml (½–¾ tsp) *cayenne* pepper
150 ml (¼ pint/⅔ cup) water
60–75 ml (4–5 tbsp) parsley, chopped

Rinse and season the prepared fish. Sauté the onions in the hot oil in a wide saucepan until light golden. Add the tomato purée, *cayenne*, water and parsley. Stir and let it bubble gently for 5 minutes. Lay the fish in the pan and cover with the sauce. Cover and cook gently for 20 minutes or slightly longer for thicker fish.

Serves 4.

KARYTHOPITTA
Walnut Pie

We sat in a row under his tent, drinking coffee and rum and eating walnuts. . . . Though not so rich as Akrivakes, he gave us water in a silver cup, which was a marvel of art. The Byzantine double-eagle, two snakes, a lion and other emblems were embossed round the rim on the bottom . . .

('GREEK LIFE IN TOWN AND COUNTRY', William Miller, George Newnes Ltd., London 1905.)

A traditional Greek gesture, as soon as a visitor arrives, particularly at island or country households, is to offer him a tiny glass of brandy, with the bouquet of the muscatel grape, a small plate of walnuts (they always seem to go with the brandy) and a small, thick,

revitalizing black coffee. At the height of the summer, when the glorious fresh fruit preserves have been safely deposited into jars, you may be offered instead a perfectly round, fresh green walnut in its heavenly sweet syrup, balancing expertly on a little silver spoon and accompanied by a cool glass of water. Walnuts in one form or another are everywhere in Greece and make their most splendid appearance in this regal, honey-moist dessert.

Karythopitta is undoubtedly the most representative of Greek desserts; either lightly spiced with the exoticism of oriental cloves and cinnamon or sparkling with the fragrance of the orange groves with its grated zest of sweetly scented oranges. Light and springy, it is finally crowned with a velvety thick, nectar-like syrup.

———— ♦ ————

150 g (5 oz) butter
100 g (4 oz/½ cup) caster (superfine) sugar
4 eggs
150 g (5 oz/1¼ cups) self-raising (self-rising) flour
2.5 ml (½ tsp) ground cinnamon
1.25 ml (¼ tsp) ground cloves

45–60 ml (3–4 tbsp) brandy
275 g (10 oz) walnuts, coarsely chopped
SYRUP
225 g (8 oz/1 cup) sugar
300 ml (½ pint/1⅓ cups) water
2–3 cloves
1 stick cinnamon
30 ml (2 tbsp) brandy

———— ♦ ————

Oven: 190°C/375°F/Mark 5.

Cream butter and sugar until light and fluffy. Add the egg yolks one by one with a pinch of flour, beating between each addition. Add the brandy and walnuts by hand because if a food processor is used at this stage it will pulverize the walnuts and the *karythopitta* will lose its character. Sift the flour with a pinch of salt and the spices. Whisk the egg whites until stiff and start folding them in with a metal spoon, alternating with tablespoons of flour, until they have all been incorporated.

Butter a medium-sized roasting tin (you need one that is quite deep as the pieces should be about 5 cm (2 in) thick), and pour the thick mixture into it, spreading it evenly. Cook in the pre-heated oven for 40 minutes.

Prepare the syrup in the meantime. Dissolve the sugar in the water, add the rest of the ingredients and boil for 8–10 minutes, until lightly thickened. Cut the *karythopitta* into diamond or square shapes in its container, without lifting out the pieces at this stage. Strain and pour the hot syrup slowly all over the cool *karythopitta*. Let it stand for 10–15 minutes to absorb all the syrup and become springy. Lift out pieces individually and arrange on a platter. Keep it covered to prevent it from drying out, if you are not going to eat it on the same day.

Serves 6–8.

SOFRITO
Veal Casserole

Sofrito is one of the best-known Corfiot dishes. The visitor will encounter it daily in the restaurants as well as in homes and as one might guess there are as many versions as there are cooks on the island. The cook presiding over his steaming kitchen at the crowded *Rex* restaurant in Kappodistriou Street, for instance, uses garlic and vinegar while the cook at the nearby *Aegli* uses onion, white wine and brandy. Mrs Zohios uses white wine and lemon and so on. The following recipe comes from Mrs Lela Makri and seemed to combine all the traditional ingredients.

Sofrito is a dish that indisputably stems from the island's Venetian past. It is served either with mashed potatoes or fried potatoes and a salad.

---

700 g (1½ lb), small thin veal slices
50 g (2 oz/6 tbsp) plain (all-purpose) flour
75 ml (5 tbsp) olive oil
30 ml (2 tbsp) white wine vinegar

3 cloves garlic, peeled and finely sliced
75 ml (5 tbsp) finely chopped parsley
450 ml (¾ pint/1¾ cups) beef stock
salt and white pepper

Coat the meat lightly with flour. Brown on both sides in the hot oil in a frying pan until pale gold. When all the pieces are browned, pour over the vinegar. When the steam subsides, take the meat out and put it in a wide saucepan with some of the oil from the pan, being careful to avoid any brown sediment. Add the remaining ingredients, cover and cook gently for 45 minutes, until the meat is tender and the sauce lightly thickened.

Serves 6.

GIOUVETSI
Baked Lamb with Pasta

Undoubtedly one of the most popular island dishes, reserved for family celebrations, such as name days (the equivalent of birthdays), baptisms or religious celebrations. It can be made with young goat, lamb or tender beef. Once the pasta is cooked, it should be consumed immediately. Sometimes, grated *kefalotyri* cheese is sprinkled on top, but I prefer it without.

1.6 kg (3½ lb) boned leg of lamb, thickly sliced
3 cloves garlic, peeled and halved
150 ml (¼ pint/⅔ cup) hot water
396 g (14 oz) tin (can) of tomatoes or 500 g (1 lb) fresh tomatoes, peeled and finely chopped
90 ml (6 tbsp) olive oil

15 ml (1 tbsp) dried oregano or the Greek *rigani*
salt and black pepper
400 g (14 oz) *orzo* (small tear-shaped pasta), the Greek *kritharaki*, which for special occasions is still home-made, or *spaghetti*, broken a little

---

Oven: 220°C/425°F/Mark 7.

Wipe the meat clean and place it in a large roasting dish with the garlic and the water. Pour over the olive oil, the tomatoes, the seasoning, and lastly the oregano.

Cook for 50 minutes, basting from time to time, and turning the pieces over. Add 300 ml (½ pint/1⅓ cups) more boiling water and mix in the pasta. Add more seasoning, turn the oven down to 200°C/400°F/Mark 6 and bake for 40 more minutes until the pasta is cooked to your taste, stirring occasionally. If needed, add a little more hot water. If using beef it would need to be cooked longer initially and with more water, until almost tender, before the pasta is added to the dish.

Serves 6.

INDEX

ACKNOWLEDGEMENTS

In doing this book, I have had the fortune to fulfill one of my dreams; that is to write about the Greek islands – small and mostly barren rocks – which have always been close to my heart.

This book is the fruitful result of our joyous journey and all its happy encounters; a token of the warm hospitality of all the people we met, friends and strangers alike. They all became friends by the end!

To give a list of everyone we met in our travels would be an impossible task but both Linda and I would like to mention a few of them, by no means in order of preference. Firstly my sisters Maria Metillia and Sally Fokianithou in Athens who were so hospitable and made our stay such an enjoyable event in between goings and comings to the islands like Ulysses. And then starting with Santorini, Maroulia Fytrou-Laoutha and her husband who made our stay such a happy event. Also in Santorini, Mrs Nitsa Pitsikali, her daughter Christina and her son George Petrakis for all the information and animated evenings they organised. In Mykonos, Mrs Taro Roussounellou and her family and Mrs Irini Monoyiou; also Anna Londou who runs the sumptuous hotel "Despotika" for her unique hospitality. In Rhodes, the hospitable Katsimbrakis brothers, Michael Koumbiathis and Mrs Maroula Hrisovergi from the village of Afandou; in Karpathos, the Despot of the island: also Mrs Maria Margariti and Mrs Stamatia Hatzikoutsou, Kostas Konthylis and particularly Elia Zervouthaki and his wife Demetra. In Kerkyra, Kosta and Spyrithoula Zohiou and their daughters. My friend Dionysis Glykopantis and his mother from Kefallonia, and my friends Chryssa and Dionysis Kouniakis from Lefkas.

All my friends in Greece who have enthusiastically offered suggestions and introductions to their friends; and particularly all our friends on Alonnisos. And I would like to thank Linda Smith for sitting patiently through endless discussions, all carried out in Greek, and animated events which must have been puzzling (to say the least) at times. Also for not being daunted by strange dishes at people's homes.

Lastly, but most importantly, we would like to thank our editors at Ebury Press, Suzanne Webber and Fiona MacIntyre, and art director Frank Phillips, without whose warm enthusiasm on the project and their encouragement in between our travels, the book would not have materialised.

Finally, Linda would like to specially thank her husband, Jonathan Sainsbury, and her parents, Barbara and Ron Smith, for their unique support and encouragement.

RENA SALAMAN
LINDA SMITH